DUE

Handy Things to Have Around the House

Handy Things to Have Around the House

Loris S. Russell

McGraw-Hill Ryerson Limited

Toronto   Montreal   New York   St. Louis
San Francisco   Auckland   Bogotá   Guatemala   Hamburg
Johannesburg   Lisbon   London   Madrid
Mexico   New Delhi   Panama   Paris   San Juan
São Paulo   Singapore   Sydney   Tokyo

Handy Things to Have Around the House

ISBN 0-07-082781-8

1 2 3 4 5 6 7 8 9 10 D 8 7 6 5 4 3 2 1 0 9

Printed and bound in Canada

Canadian Cataloguing in Publication Data

Russell, Loris S., date
    Handy things to have around the house

Bibliography: p.
Includes index.
ISBN 0-07-082781-8

1. Household appliances — History — 19th century.
I. Title.

TX298.R87   643'.6'09034   C79-094523-1

Contents

Acknowledgements

Many persons have helped in the preparation of this account by providing information or access to specimens. To Mr. Russell K. Cooper, Administrator of the Historical Sites Division, The Metropolitan Toronto and Region Conservation Authority, special thanks are due not only for such assistance, but also for encouragement to proceed with the project and enthusiasm for its results. Black Creek Pioneer Village comes under Mr. Cooper's jurisdiction, and here I have been greatly assisted by Mr. Harold Lund, former curator of the collection, who patiently made available the objects that I wished to study and photograph. More recently his successor, Mrs. Margaret Hesp, has been equally helpful.

Mr. Albert Colucci, formerly of Black Pioneer Village, and later with the Ontario Science Centre, provided access to objects under his care and advice on their significance. Study of material in the numerous restorations maintained by the Toronto Historical Board was possible through the courtesy of Brigadier General J. A. McGinnis, Managing Director. Mrs. Dorothy Duncan, formerly with the Historical Board, now Museums Advisor to the Heritage Administration, Ontario Department of Culture and Recreation, provided information on objects in the historical houses. At the Royal Ontario Museum, Mr. Donald Webster, who originally suggested this study, made available holdings in the Canadiana Department, of which he is Curator. Miss Edith Firth, Head of the Canadian History Department, Metropolitan Toronto Library Board, provided valuable guidance, as well as access to the holdings of her department. Mrs. Nancy Gloger, Assistant Librarian of the Consumers' Gas Company, Toronto, supplied information and records on 19th-century gas fixtures and stoves.

At Ottawa, Dr. W. E. Taylor, Director of the Museum of Man, National Museums of Canada, authorized access to the collections, and the Chief of the History Division, Dr. F. J. Thorpe, with his staff, was most helpful in the use of the objects under his care.

In Washington, D.C., Mr. C. Malcolm Watkins, of the National Museum of History and Technology, permitted access to the reserve collection of domestic appliances. Ms. Grace R. Cooper, Curator of Textiles, made possible the photographing of many early sewing machines, as well as supplying official photographs of others.

The outstanding collection of the Greenfield Village and Henry Ford Museum at Dearborn, Michigan, was made available by Dr. Kenneth M. Wilson, Director of Collections and Preservation. Miss Donna Rosenstein, of his staff, assisted in the study and photographing of objects. Mr. Edward R. Kukla, formerly Assistant Librarian, Rare Books and Manuscripts, Henry Ford Museum, provided access to early encyclopedias and trade catalogues, and later made photocopies available. Subsequently, Miss Joan W. Gartland, Librarian of the Henry Ford Museum, arranged for additional photographs to be provided.

Other libraries in the United States provided photocopies of catalogues, advertisements, and biographical sketches among their holdings. Particularly helpful were Mr. Anthony A. Roth, The Historical Society of Pennsylvania, Philadelphia; Miss Ruth Marshall, Boston Public Library; Miss Donna F. Williams, Lowell City Library, Lowell, Massachusetts; Miss Nancy E. Gaudette, Worcester Public Library, Worcester, Mass.; and Mr. Lawrence Brengle, Leominster Public Library, Leominster, Mass.

Photographs credited to the Royal Ontario Museum were taken by Mr. Leigh R. Warren, Head Photographer, and his staff. On one occasion Mr. Warren travelled with me to Fenelon Falls, Ontario, to photograph the Anne Langton sketches preserved in the Library and Museum there.

Special thanks are due to my wife, Grace Evelyn Russell, who has been my companion and supporter in this as well as other antiquarian projects. Her knowledge of old-time domestic practices through youthful observations and family tradition has enabled her to provide much helpful advice and criticism.

Note: Unless otherwise stated, photographs were taken by the author.

L.S.R.

Introduction

The 19th century was the age of household gadgets. Mechanical devices to make domestic tasks less laborious or more successful increased from a few simple aids to an elaborate array of ingenious hardware rivalling a workshop or a laboratory. This multiplication of household accessories spilled over into the 20th century and exploded in a thousand marvels of electrical engineering, but in the 19th century the improvement of domestic equipment was something new. The techniques and appliances of the home had changed little in western European culture since the days of King Alfred. In fact, the good king of Wessex could have burned the cakes just as easily at an 18th-century fireplace as at a 9th-century hearth. But by the late 1700s changes were underway. The American and French revolutions had asserted the importance of the common man. The spirit of scientific enquiry, hitherto confined to an elite, was seeping down to the middle classes. People were becoming receptive to new ideas; what was good enough for their grandfathers was not necessarily the optimum for them.

This awakening of interest in what was new provided at last a favorable environment for the inventor. In England the granting of letters patent (public recognition of an invention) went back to 1617, but in the late 1700s there began to be some hope that the products of invention would find a rewarding market. With this incentive the applications for patents began to increase by multiplication. Each new invention led to a series of "improvements". In America the granting of patents had begun under British rule, but with independence the United States Patent Office was established in 1790. It escaped the burning of public buildings in Washington during the 1814 raid, only to be destroyed by fire in 1836. From this disaster it arose Phoenix-like to a more effective organization. The British North American colonies of Lower and Upper Canada established a patent office in 1824. It is of interest that the first Canadian patent was for a "washing and fulling machine".

The increase in the number of patents issued in the United States and Canada during the second quarter of the 19th century was dramatic. In 1825 the U.S. Patent Office isued 245 patents;[1] in 1850 the number was 995.[2] The corresponding figures for the "Canadas" (Quebec and Ontario) were 1 and 34.[3] Many of these patents were for improved domestic appliances, such as meat choppers, sausage stuffers, churns, washing machines, and stoves. Although some of these new devices were made elsewhere, the market for household gadgetry became more and more dominated by the New England manufacturers. The ingenious Yankee inventor appeared as a traditional figure, immortalized by Mark Twain in his "Connecticut Yankee in King Arthur's Court", but in reality there were just as many new ideas coming from New York State and the middle west. It was the abundance of water power in New England that brought about the concentration of American manufactory there in the first half of the 19th century. As the steam engine succeeded the water wheel, industry moved westward. Pennsylvania and upstate New York, with closer access to the great coal fields, became rivals of the New England states in light as well as heavy industry. In 1854 free trade was established between the United States and Canada, and the products of U.S. factories quickly secured much of the market for manufactured goods north of the border. "Yankee" appliances and implements became the stock in trade of the retail merchant and the peddlar.

This 19th-century enthusiasm for improved domestic devices has been ascribed to the increasing difficulty in hiring domestic servants as opportunities for other employment became more available. This no doubt was an important factor; the housewife, faced unaided with the domestic chores, might be eager to adopt easier and better ways of doing them. But this was more an excuse than a reason. There was the same acceptance of better techniques and appliances in non-domestic activities, and in western Europe as well as North America. People were becoming greatly impressed with the achievements of the new technology. The steam engine, the gas light, the electromagnetic telegraph, were such obvious and magnificent contributions to the better life that novelty was coming to be equated with desirability. The old suspicion of the new was giving way to an eagerness to try it. And the more successful the new device, the greater the readiness to accept the next innovation. This trend was most obvious in the major industries, such as agriculture and manufacturing, but the manner in which it changed the domestic regime is the subject of the present account.

Sources

For the study of material culture within historic times the sources consist of the written record and the surviving objects. The synthesis of these two kinds of evidence permits a reconstruction of the material resources of a period and the manner in which those resources were used.

In the present study, which deals with the appliances of 19th-century domestic economy, the most authoritative documents are the letters patent for those appliances. The United States Patent Office has in printed form the specifications and drawings of all its patents issued since 1836. The resources of this great collection, and the courtesy of its staff, have been greatly appreciated. Of the "name and date" patents that survived the fire of 1836, photocopies are available from the U.S. National Archives and Records Service, Washington, D.C.

The Canadian Patent Office, Department of Consumer and Corporate Affairs, Ottawa, preserves the originals of all Canadian patents since 1824, as well as those of other British North American colonies prior to Confederation. Until 1855, summaries of patents were printed in the series Patents of Canada, but printing of Canadian patents was then suspended until 1873, when volume 1 of the Canadian Patent Office Record was issued, and these have continued. The Canadian Patent Office also has a nearly complete series of the printed specifications of U.S. patents, as well as those of Great Britain and other countries.

In some instances the patent records preserved in Toronto libraries have been sufficient for the present study. The library of the University of Toronto has a nearly complete series of the Annual Reports, U.S. Commissioner of Patents, 1847 to 1868. Issues of this series from 1850 to 1871, followed by a complete set of the Index and Gazette, are also represented in the collection of the Metropolitan Toronto Library Board. Another good series, 1872 to the present, has been consulted in the Great Hall Library, Osgoode Hall, Toronto.

The limitation of patents as historical records is that they provide no evidence as to the extent to which the object of the patent was manufactured and used, or even if it were ever produced commercially at all. This gap is best filled by the object itself, but next to that, the catalogues of manufacturers and dealers are the most helpful, especially if dated. Many such catalogues, either as originals or photocopies, were consulted in the present project. Others are available in printed facsimile, and these are listed in the bibliography.

The numerous memoirs and letters left by 19th-century observers do not provide much information on the domestic arts and appliances of their times. More useful to this project have been the books written by experienced ladies for the guidance of young women setting up a domestic establishment and practising the household arts. Along with good advice on management and behavior, these works discuss the material resources of the home, with comments on their advantages and limitations. A selection of such works consulted appears in the bibliography.

Excellent books by modern authors have provided information and leads that have been used and expanded upon. Because it approaches most nearly the subject of the present work, the most useful has been the well-illustrated volume "America in the Kitchen from Hearth to Cookstove", by Linda Campbell Franklin. Very different in format but almost as helpful in this area is Earl Lifshey's "The Housewares Story", which brings the history of domestic appliances well into the 20th century. Other works of a similar nature but of more occasional application are cited in the text and listed in the bibliography.

Many fine collections of domestic appliances exist in the United States and Canada, and ideally all would have been consulted. Limitations of time and space have restricted me to the collections near at hand. Of these, the most important is that of the National Museums of Canada, Museum of Man, Ottawa. This collection, in the History Division, was begun under my direction and expanded since. It covers the entire range of objects used in Canada in the arts and trades. Another collection used extensively in the present project is that of Black Creek Pioneer Village, Toronto, established and maintained by the Metropolitan Toronto and Region Conservation Authority. The extent to which these two collections have been used by me can be judged from the credit lines of the accompanying illustrations.

Other museums and historic restorations in the Toronto area have been drawn upon for information, and their collections studied. These include the Royal Ontario Museum (Canadiana Department), the Ontario Science Centre, and the restorations of the Toronto Historical Board — Fort York, Mackenzie House and Gibson House.* Elsewhere in Ontario important objects were studied at Doon Pioneer Village near Kitchener, Upper Canada Village near Morrisburg, the Hiram Walker Historical Museum at Windsor, the Guelph Civic Museum at Guelph, the Niagara Historical Society Museum at Niagara-on-the-Lake, and the Mackenzie House at Queenston. Other Canadian museums that were helpful to this project are the Nova Scotia Museum in Halifax and the New Brunswick Museum in Saint John.

Of the many historical museums in the United States, by far the most useful to this study has been the Greenfield Village and Henry Ford Museum at Dearborn, Michigan. Not only is this a leading museum for the history of technology, but most of its holdings are on display. The enlightened motives that led Mr. Ford to establish this great institution and his successors to maintain it have made it a mecca for those interested in the history of material culture. It is hoped that the Henry Ford Museum never succumbs to the modern tendency of historical museums to restrict themselves to thematic and didactic exhibits.

The most prestigious collection of historic artifacts in the United States is that of the Smithsonian Institution, National Museum of History and Technology, Washington, D.C. Here may be seen on exhibition or in the systematic collection much of the material from the old Patent Office Museum, and many objects from the Centennial Exhibition of 1876. Many of the holdings have intrinsic historical as well as technological importance. Examples are the sewing machines of Howe and Singer and the telegraph instruments of Samuel Morse. It has been a privilege to study many of these objects in detail.

The Shelburne Museum, Shelburne, Vermont, has an outstanding collection of household objects, mostly from the first half of the 19th century. Other collections of importance to the present study are those of Old Sturbridge Village, Sturbridge, Massachusetts; and the Pennsylvania Farm Museum of Landis Valley, Lancaster, Pennsylvania. Many other history museums, from Florida on the south to Texas on the west, have been visited briefly, and their pertinent holdings noted. Space does not permit listing these, but a collective note of appreciation is offered to all those enthusiastic museum workers and collectors who are helping to preserve the record of material history in the United States and Canada.

---

* Gibson House is now the responsibility of the North York Historical Board.

1

The Fireplace Kitchen

The fireplace was the direct descendant of the campfire, and the techniques of cooking that went with it were not much different from those of the tribal hearth. Until the 1840s or later the open fireplace was almost the universal means of cooking. By the beginning of the century, however, some sophisticated devices were coming into use for fireplace cooking, and had not the cooking stove taken over, they might have reached a high degree of complexity.

The primary function of the fireplace was the provision of warmth, and so it was a basic part of each dwelling, incorporated at the time of building. In its usual form it was a large recess in one wall, the floor and lining of which were of stone or brick. A simple but dangerous form of construction was a wooden framework covered with clay; this might be used in the temporary dwellings of settlers. Similarly, make-shift fireplaces were built without chimneys, the smoke escaping, more or less, through crevices in the roof and walls. But in a sophisticated fireplace a well designed chimney was an essential part. It was not only a means of escape for smoke, but by concentrating the rising hot air and fumes, it created a draft that increased the oxygen supply to the fire. Unfortunately, not all builders understood the principles of fireplace design, and the smoking fireplace was all too common.

A well designed kitchen fireplace (Fig. 1) might be six or more feet in width, with the opening three or four feet wide and at least three feet deep. Some fireplaces were much larger, like miniature rooms, with enough space at one side for a bench on which people could sit and warm themselves on coming in from the cold outside.

Fig. 1. *Restored fireplace kitchen, Officers' Quarters, Fort York, Toronto, Ontario.*

Fig. 2. Fireplace, Gibson House, Willowdale, Ontario.

The Fire

The chimney opening ideally was above and a little to the rear of the actual hearth, and tapered from the full width of the chamber to that of the chimney. However, a tapered flue was hard to build and more often the opening was a simple rectangle, the same dimensions as the chimney. Such a flue was likely to allow the escape of smoke into the kitchen.

Late 18th and early 19th century kitchen fireplaces usually had an oven incorporated in one of the walls (Fig. 2). This was a small chamber, opening to the front or perhaps into the fireplace, and at a convenient height from the floor. It had its own flue, and perhaps an opening for ash disposal. Often it had a cast-iron door.

Fireplace fuel was normally wood. Logs were chopped or sawn to lengths somewhat less than the width of the fireplace, and split to convenient thicknesses. The fresh wood surface ignited more easily than the bark. For a quick, hot fire, soft wood such as pine or poplar was best. Hardwood lasted longer but was more difficult to ignite. Kindling was made by cutting slivers of wood with axe or knife, or by whittling shavings from the edge of a stick.

Until the appearance of chemical matches early in the 19th century, fire lighting was almost universally by means of "flint and steel" (Fig. 3). In this technique, incandescent sparks were struck from a bar of steel by blows from a piece of flint or other

Fig. 3. Flint and steel with tinder, sulphur splints, and tinder box. LSR Collection.

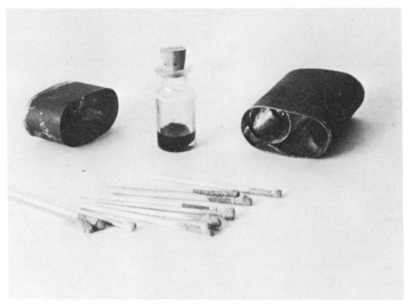

Fig. 4. Instantaneous light outfit: matches, acid bottle, and container. LSR Collection.

siliceous rock. The equipment was usually housed in a tinder box, a low cylindrical can, the lid of which might have a socket for a candle. The "steel" or "strike-a-light" was a short bar of steel, perhaps made from a discarded file. A wrought-iron handle was welded on at one or both ends. The "flint" might be a discarded gun flint, although a larger piece was more effective. The third essential ingredient was tinder, made by scorching strips of linen almost to the charcoal condition.

In use, the steel was held vertically over the can containing the tinder. The edge of the steel was struck with the flint in downward glancing blows. Tiny sparks would fall from the steel onto the tinder, and with luck would ignite the linen to produce a spreading ember. To transform this into a flame it was easiest to use a sulphur match or splint, a flat sliver of wood several inches long, the ends coated by dipping into molten sulphur. One of these sulphur tips was touched against the glowing tinder, and with some blowing, could be made to burst into flame.

Lighting a fire with flint and steel was a tedious operation at best, and almost impossible if the tinder was damp from humidity. To avoid having to relight the fire on the following morning, the remnants of the day's fire might be preserved by banking the coals with ashes, but if this failed, someone would go to a more fortunate neighbor to obtain glowing coals, brought back on a shovel or in a special ember box with a long handle and a sliding lid.

The invention of chemical matches early in the 19th century marked the beginning of the end of fire-making by flint and steel.[1] The earliest of these, the Chancel or instantaneous match (Fig. 4), was a small stick of wood about the size of a modern wooden match. One end was impregnated with sulphur and then dipped in a paste made of potassium chlorate, powdered sugar, and glue. The other part of the kit was a small jar containing a little concentrated sulphuric acid ("oil of vitriol"). To ignite the match, the head was dipped into the acid, then quickly withdrawn, whereupon it would burst into flame. Instantaneous match kits came in a small sheet-metal box containing the acid jar and the matches.

Chancel matches were introduced about 1805, but their use spread slowly. They were messy, and the acid deteriorated on exposure to air. A more practical type of match was invented in 1826 by an English apothecary, James Walker. The Walker match (Fig. 5) was a flat stick, one end of which was coated with a mixture of potassium chlorate and antimony pentoxide. The latter ingredient gave the head its characteristic orange color. To ignite the match, the head was pinched in a folded piece of sandpaper, then quickly pulled out. Walker matches were sold under the name of friction light or Lucifer match. Compared with modern matches, they were difficult to ignite.

A simpler and more practical friction match was introduced in the 1830s. In this the head consisted of a mixture of white

Fig. 5. Walker friction matches (reconstructed), LSR Collection.

phosphorus and sulphur. Although of Austrian origin, these "strike-anywhere" matches were made and widely sold by English manufacturers under the name of Congreve matches. They came in ornate boxes (Fig. 6) or metal containers, and quickly became the almost universal means of fire making in North America.

The final development of the friction match occurred in 1855 with the invention by J. E. Lundstrom of Sweden of the safety or Swedish match. In this the active ingredients were separated, the head consisting of potassium chlorate, potassium dichromate, and other compounds, the friction surface of antimony trisulphide, and other substances. Neither mixture by itself could be ignited by friction, but striking one against the other would cause the match head to burst into flame. Safety matches based on this invention are still being widely used.

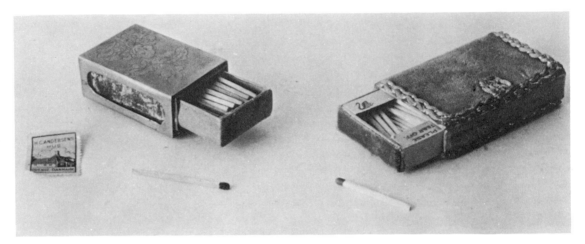

Fig. 6. Nineteenth-century match boxes, LSR Collection.

Fireplace Equipment

Food could be cooked at a fireplace in one of three ways: by suspending it free or in a container over the fire; by supporting it in front of the fire, with or without a heat reflector; by placing it in an oven on the side of the fireplace, which was preheated with its own fire or with live coals.

Probably the most atavistic utensil used in fireplace cooking was the *spit,* which was not much removed from the pointed stick that held a piece of meat over a camp fire. By the 18th century the fireplace spit consisted of an iron rod, pointed at one end and with a crank and handle at the other. It rested horizontally on two supports, one at each end. In use the meat was skewered on the rod, more or less in the middle, and the whole device set close enough to the open fire that the near side of the meat would be roasted. Intermittent turning of the crank insured that all sides of the meat were uniformly cooked. Turning the spit was not only tedious, it was also uncomfortable for the operator to be so close to the heat. The latter problem could be partly solved by extending the handle end of the rod far enough to one side to be out of the hot area. Another method was to connect the spit bar to the crank by means of pulleys or gears. In some kitchens the spit was attached to a dog tread-mill (Fig. 7).

The *clock jack* was a mechancial device to turn meat while it was being roasted. Some rare examples have the mechanism attached to a horizontal spit. Usually it hung vertically over the fire, with the meat suspended by one or more hooks below. A powerful spring motor in the jack turned the meat through part of a circle, first in one direction, then in the other. Most clock jacks were made in

England. They usually are in the form of a brass cylinder (Fig. 8), about four inches in diameter and seven inches high. Within this is the spring motor. A brass tube extends from the top for about eight inches, with a metal loop for hanging. A hook projects from the bottom of the cylinder. After the spring had been wound with the key provided, and the device hung over the fire, meat was attached to the lower hook. In another version (Fig. 9) the mechanism is in a short, wide cylinder, like a modern table clock. The example shown bears on its face the royal arms and the following inscription: T. RESTELL'S PATENT / WARRANTED / SOLE MANU-FACTURERS / E. B. BENNET & SONS.

In order to broil more than one piece of meat at a time, clock jacks were provided with a cast-iron, wheel-like accessory, which could be suspended at the centre on the jack hook. Rings hanging from the "wheel" permitted several pieces of meat to be attached

Fig. 7. Dog tread-mill and fireplace with spit, Chateau de Ramezay, Montreal.

Fig. 8. Clock-jack, National Museum of Man, Ottawa.

Fig. 9. Clock-jack, Black Creek Pioneer Village, Toronto.

by S-hooks, but the load would have to be well balanced.

The *reflector oven* (Fig. 10) was a kind of spit in which the food could be heated on all sides simultaneously. The spit bar is mounted at the axis of a semi-cylindrical sheet-metal reflector. With the open side facing the fire, heat would be reflected from the curved inner surface onto the back of the food, while direct heat cooked the front. Heating was not

a

b

Fig. 10. *Reflector oven: (a) front view; (b) in working position. Officers' Quarters, Fort York, Toronto.*

completely uniform, but near enough so that turning the spit could be occasional, rather than constant. Reflector ovens were also built with a vertical orientation. In these the spit was turned from the top. Meat could be hung from a hook, rather than impaled on a rod. But the shape of the vertical reflector did not conform as well to the shape of the fire as did the horizontal version. The origin of the reflector oven is not known, but it was in wide use by the beginning of the 19th century. Modified versions were used for roasting fowl or apples or for baking cakes in pans.

The *crane* (Fig. 11) was a device for suspending receptacles over the fire. The simplest support was a horizontal bar of iron attached at each end to the fireplace wall.

But this was incapable of movement or adjustment, and most fireplaces had a crane. It was a piece of iron shaped like an inverted letter L, the vertical arm of which fitted into rings on one wall of the fireplace, leaving the horizontal arm free to swing in an arc from a position over the fire to well out in front of the fireplace. Some cranes were ornamented with curved braces and other elaborations. Pots, kettles, skillets, and clock jacks could be suspended from the crane by means of S-hooks or trammels.

The *trammel* was a utensil that permitted varying the height of the suspended vessel over the fire, even though the height of the crane was fixed. Large trammels (Fig. 12) were also used with out-of-doors fires to

Fig. 11. Reconstructed fireplace with crane, National Museum of Man, Ottawa.

suspend the huge pots used in potash-making and maple-syrup boiling. The trammel looks like a saw with large teeth. Actually the "teeth" are stops, like those of a ratchet-wheel; the upper side of each projection is at right angles to the vertical axis of the trammel. The upper end has a hook or eye for attachment to the crane. The part corresponding to the ratchet is a rod with a loop at the upper end and a hook at the lower. The loop can be engaged with any of the "teeth", thus making it possible to select the height of the hook and its suspended container above the fire.

Pots (Fig. 13) were of cast iron and were either round or flat bottomed. The round pot was better for stirring the contents and for cleaning, but it had to have three short legs on the under side to rest upright on a flat surface. Pots had a wire handle by means of which they were suspended from crane or trammel. The *skillet* (Fig. 14) was like a flat-bottomed pot, but had low sides. It too was suspended in use, and served as a frying pan. *Teakettles* (Fig. 15) were bulbous pots with a lid and a curved spout. They were of heavy cast iron, but later, when sheet-metal (tole) teakettles came into use on stoves, they retained the same shape. One ingenious

Fig. 12. Trammel on tripod, National Museum of Man, Ottawa.

Fig. 13. Iron pot, National Museum of Man, Ottawa.

Fig. 14. Hanging skillet, National Museum of Man,
        Ottawa.

Fig. 15. Iron teakettles, National Museum of Man,
        Ottawa.

Fig. 16. Double-boiler pot, National Museum of Man, Ottawa.

fireplace teakettle had a tilting device, so that it could be poured from while still suspended.

The familiar *double-boiler*, in which an upper pot with the food fits into a lower pot with boiling water, did not become practical until the solid support of the cooking stove was available. Over the open fire, similar results could be obtained by suspending one pot inside a second, larger one. A pot made especially for this purpose has a high handle with a double loop (Fig. 16). It could be attached to a crane by two S-hooks. The second pot, holding the food to be cooked, was suspended by another S-hook from the low point at the middle of the large handle.

The *trivet* was designed to support a cooking vessel over or close to the fire. The usual form is an iron ring, flat on top, and supported by three high legs. Another type, used for keeping food warm, is shelf-like, and was fitted into the wall of the fireplace. Trivets with short legs were used to support hot pans and pots on a table top.

The *spider* (Fig. 17) was another kind of frying pan. It had three high legs and was in effect a union of skillet and trivet. It provided good stability over the fire, but must have been awkward to handle. With the introduction of the cooking stove, stability was no longer a problem, and the skillet could be placed directly on the stove top or over an open pot hole.

Tongs (Fig. 18) were characteristic fireplace utensils. They served to lift embers

Fig. 17. Fireplace with pot and spider, Black Creek Pioneer Village, Toronto.

out of the fire to light a candle or a pipe, or to pick up objects dropped in the fire. They could be used to shift meat on a hot skillet, or even to adjust the position of the burning wood. The usual tongs were made of heavy iron wire or rod, coiled once at the handle end to form a spring, and with the two arms crossed at the lower end so as to cause the tips to close rather than open with the spring tension. Fire tongs were of simpler design; two straight arms hinged on each other, without a spring. Such tongs were similar to those used by blacksmiths. A special version of this type are the waffle tongs (Fig. 19). These have long handles and short jaws, the latter being in the form of rectangular or circular plates. The inner surfaces of these plates do not quite come together when closed, and they have a grid-like pattern

or an ornamental design. When the surfaces were greased, and a spoonful of batter dropped on one face, the tongs were closed, and the jaws with contents held over the fire. The batter was quickly cooked, and the hot waffle or biscuit dropped on a plate by opening the jaws. This method of cooking was used in convents to prepare the communion wafers from unleavened dough. Tongs used for this purpose have the sacred symbols on the face.

Toasting bread at an open fire could be done by holding the slice on a long-handled fork. But this is a tedious, uncomfortable method, and sometimes the slice falls into the fire. More uniform toasting, with no risk of dropping the bread, could be done on a *toasting frame* (Fig. 20). This consists of an iron base, about a foot long and two inches

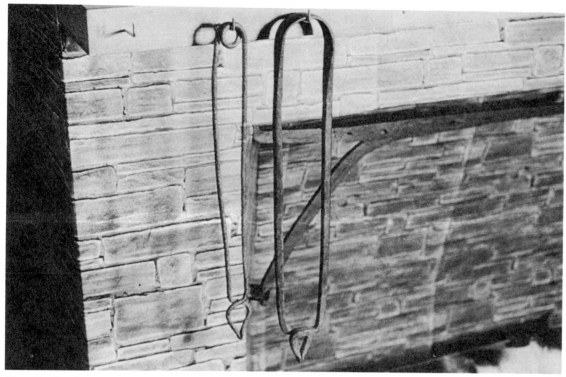

Fig. 18. *Fireplace tongs, National Museum of Man, Ottawa.*

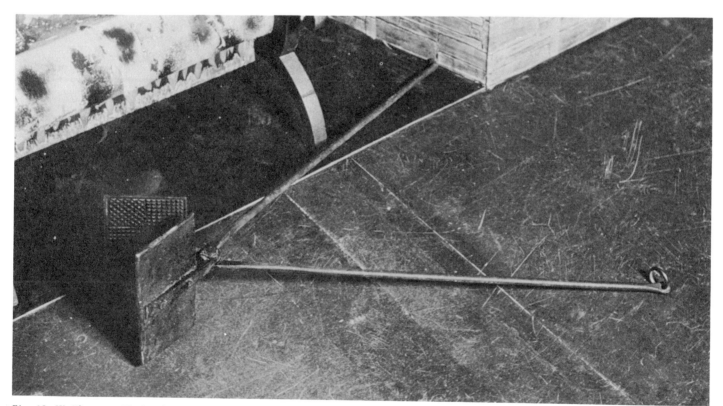

Fig. 19. *Waffle tongs, National Museum of Man, Ottawa.*

wide, supported on four short legs. From the top of the base two wire frames project upward, one from each edge, so that slices of bread dropped between the frames would be held vertically. At the centre is a swivel attachment for a long handle, which enables the toaster to be moved closer to or farther away from the fire. In some toasters the base is slightly curved, concave towards the fire, so that the slices more directly face the source of heat. Another version has the base on a central pivot, so that the toaster can be turned without removing the slices.

The *gridiron* is a frame of parallel iron bars forming a partly open platform on which meat or fish can be broiled over an open fire. In its simplest form it is an iron rectangular frame, with narrow bars joining the two sides, leaving spaces of about half an inch between bars. The frame is supported on four legs and has a handle at the middle of one side. Juices from the broiling food dropped into the fire and were lost, so in 1820 a gridiron with "guttered" bars was patented by T. Mussey of New London, Conn.[2] The miniature troughs of the bars led into a transverse channel, which drains into a small, cup-shaped receptacle. With the gridiron mounted so as to slope slightly toward the cup, any juice caught by the concave bars would accumulate in the cup, to be saved, or spooned out for basting. In this or other single-sided gridirons the food had to be turned with fork or lifter to be cooked on the other side. In 1867 E. P. Russell of Manlius, N.Y., patented[3] a closed gridiron, consisting of two frames hinged on each other at one point on the rims (Fig. 21). With the meat or

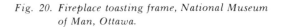

Fig. 20. Fireplace toasting frame, National Museum of Man, Ottawa.

Fig. 21. Reversible gridiron, Russell patent, National Museum of Man, Ottawa.

fish clamped between the two frames, both sides could be broiled by turning over the whole utensil at the proper moment. Such a gridiron was used on a trivet, or over the opening in a stove top.

The *coffee roaster* was a familiar piece of fireplace paraphernalia, and in modified form persisted into the cooking stove era. Until about the middle of the 19th century, when commercial-scale coffee roasters became available, coffee was sold as whole green beans. The roasting was done at home, possibly in a skillet or pot over the fire. To avoid under-roasting or burning, the beans had to be agitated by stirring or shaking. This could be tedious and uncomfortable. A more efficient method was needed, and so in 1820, P. Williamson of Baltimore, Md., patented[4] a mechancial coffee roaster. Unfortunately no copy of this patent is extant, but it was probably like later versions, a kind of rotary spit. A sheet-iron can, about seven inches long and five inches in diameter, is mounted axially on an iron rod, which rests horizontally on spit-like supports. The can has a hinged, curved lid on the side, which can be secured when closed. The raw coffee beans were placed in the can, the lid closed, and the device set up in front of the fire and turned with a handle at one end. Some roasting cans were made to be mounted on the meat spit. Completion of roasting was indicated by the change in color of the beans from grey-green to a uniform dark brown. The characteristic aroma was also an indication.

Baking at the fireplace was usually done in an oven in the side wall (Fig. 22), although in some places such as rural Quebec, out-of-doors ovens were commonly used. In either case the oven was heated by building in it, or introducing into it a fire, which was removed when the proper temperature was reached. The pans of dough were then set in the oven, usually by hand, but to remove the baked loaves a utensil was needed. This was the *peel*, a kind of flat shovel of wood, iron, or a combination of metal blade and wooden handle. Some cooks placed the lumps of dough on a greased metal plate, without pan, but even in this method the peel was useful in removing or shifting the loaves.

Fig. 22. Fireplace oven, Officers' Quarters, Fort York,
   Toronto.

The Cooking Stove

2

The great revolution in domestic economy during the 19th century was the introduction of the cooking stove. Records of the time do not recognize the great change that was taking place, for it was a gradual one. It began in the 1830s, but had not reached the more remote parts of North America even in the 1870s. It was, however, the most drastic of all steps taken to reduce the housewife's drudgery.

The invention of the cooking stove is sometimes credited to Benjamin Thompson, Count Rumford, but his was a large construction, designed more for the barracks than the home.[1] The domestic cooking stove was derived from two sources, more or less independently. One was the fireplace, the other the heating stove, and designs from the two sources were distinct. The fireplace cooking stove began with an iron plate stretched across the hearth, an oven at one end and a tank for hot water at the other. The next step was the closing of the fireplace front, leaving a door for fuel and ash removal, and openings for ventilation. This type of stove was called a range, and it soon reached a high state of sophistication, with ingenious arrangements of the flues to obtain maximum use of the heat. One of the early U.S. patents[2] for a range was issued in 1837 to John Morris, of Derby, Connecticut. In his stove the fire box portion projected forward in a curved shape, with three separate chambers connected to a single flue, and capable of being operated singly or together. The oven was situated in a plate built into the fireplace above the fire boxes, and was heated by the ascending hot air and smoke. Provision was made for a roaster in front and a broiler on top.

A curious fireplace range was patented[3] in 1839 by Eldridge McCollum, of Weare, New Hampshire. This had two cylindrical ovens, one on either side of the semi-cylindrical fire box. In the 1840s the range was characteristic of the more elaborate domestic establishments, such as those in which a special room, usually in the basement, was set aside exclusively as the kitchen. A fine example (Fig. 23) may be seen in the William Lyon Mackenzie House in Toronto, Ontario, which is restored and refurnished to represent its appearance in the 1850s.

Heating stoves of iron were brought to North America from Europe early in the 18th century, and their manufacture was begun soon after in both the English and French colonies. Some of these early stoves had no flue, the smoke having to find its way up the fireplace chimney. They were all made of flat iron plates with or without ornamentation, and were fitted together by means of interlocking edges (Fig. 24). In the 19th century these box stoves were elaborated upon by adding one or two chambers above the fire box; this increased the distribution of heat and provided warming space for food, but did not make them suitable for cooking.

The conversion of the box-shaped heating stove into a cooking stove began early in the 19th century. The earliest U.S. patent[4] for such an improvement was issued in 1812 to J. Low of Fitzhugh, Massachusetts. Most of these early stoves had a fire box, an attached oven (usually in the rear), and a top with openings for direct cooking. A prophetic design was patented[5] and manufactured in 1835 by Joseph Van Norman of Normandale, Upper Canada. In this the fire box was on the left, the oven and flue on the right, and the top was provided with four large openings with lids. A fine example (Fig. 25) of this earliest of Canadian cooking stoves is preserved in the Mackenzie House at Queenston, Ontario. It is the basic design of many cooking stoves both American and Canadian in the 19th and on into the 20th century.

Fig. 23. Kitchen range in Mackenzie House, Toronto.

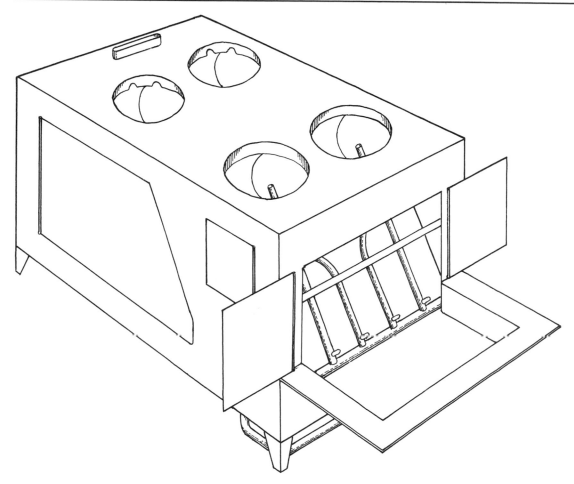

Fig. 29. Gas cooking stove, Sanderson patent, 1867. Drawing by LSR, based on the patent drawing. Note the four feed pipes for the "pot holes" *and the separate pipe below for the oven.*

as that still in use (Fig. 29). It was box-like, with four openings for pots in the top and an oven below. Each pot opening, as well as the oven, had its own gas jet, the flow to which was controlled by an individual stop-cock, with the air for the flame being provided through side openings in each pipe.

The gas stove, unlike the solid-fuel stove, needed no fire box. The cooking vessels were set over the open flame, usually supported by a cast-iron grill. Cooking was fast and temperature control easy; there was greater comfort for the user in the reduction of radiated heat, and convenience in not having to carry in fuel and take out ashes. In spite of these advantages, gas stoves were slow in gaining acceptance. For one thing, they could be used only in communities where a gas-distribution system was already in existence.

In order to overcome prejudice and make the gas stove more acceptable, models were introduced that could burn gas, coal, or wood. By the 1880s, gas used for cooking and heating was an important part of the output of gas companies, which was a good thing for them, as the electric arc and the carbon-filament electric light were beginning to displace gas burners as the source of street and domestic illumination. In some fortunate areas, such as western Pennsylvania and southwestern Ontario, drilling for oil in the 1880s led to the discovery of natural gas in sufficient quantities to provide a cheap substitute for artificial gas for heating as well as lighting. Gas cooking stoves required only a minor adjustment of the burners to make them suitable for the new fuel. Even where only artificial gas was available, the

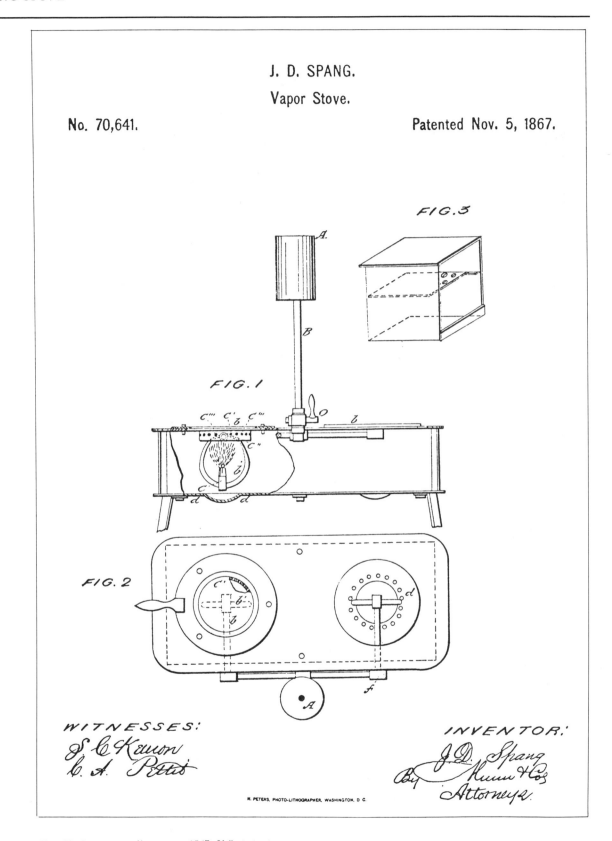

Fig. 30. Spang gasoline stove, 1867, U.S. patent
drawing.

popularity of this fuel for cooking stoves continued to grow well into the 20th century, and as the gas lamp was displaced by the electric light, the production of gas became almost entirely for the purpose of cooking and heating.

Where gas was not available, gasoline was a good substitute as fuel for cooking stoves. This highly volatile liquid was fed to the burner through a fine valve, arranged so that the flame heated the feed pipe adjacent to the valve. After an initial warming-up interval, the fuel emerged as a vapor, which provided a very hot, smokeless flame similar to that of the gas burner. The first U.S. patent[10] for a gasoline stove was issued in 1867 to Jacob D. Spang of Dayton, Ohio (Fig. 30). The drawing shows a two-burner stove, with the fuel tank well above the stove top, feeding the fuel through a pipe with a stop-cock to a vertical ring which led to the burner. There do not appear to be individual stop-cocks for each burner. By the 1890s, gasoline stoves had not changed very much. There were single, double, and triple burner models, each burner with its own control; some such stoves had a built-in oven with its own burner, others used a separate oven placed over a burner. Gasoline stoves were especially suitable for summer kitchens, as they radiated little heat and did not require a chimney. In the 20th century these stoves were elaborated by adding an air pump to the fuel tank, so that the fuel entered the burner under pressure. Stoves of this type are still widely used for camp cooking and for temporary installations as in summer cottages.

Kerosene stoves were very different from those using gas or gasoline as the fuel; they were developed from the kerosene lamp, which on occasion had doubled as a small heater. The first U.S. patent[11] for a kerosene stove was obtained by W.H. Elliott of Plattsburg, N.Y., in 1865. His was a sophisticated design, with two burners using adjustable flat wicks. The essential feature of the patent was the manner of securing the burners to the under side of the stove box. By the 1890s, kerosene stoves with oval wicks were the common type (Fig. 31). Each burner was provided with a mica ("isin-glass") window through which the adjustment of the flame could be observed. Like the gasoline stove, the kerosene stove had its use mainly for hot-weather cooking.

Stove Utensils

Some of the pots and pans designed for the fireplace could be, and surely were, used on the newly developed stove. But round-bottom pots were unsuitable and were replaced by those with flat bottoms. Skillets with handles for hanging or legs for standing were out, and the familiar frying pan, with its projecting handle, became a standard cooking-stove utensil. A true double boiler, with one pot fitting tightly into the other, was another innovation made possible by the stove. Cast-iron teakettles made for fireplaces were usable on stove tops, but a new kind appeared, in which the bottom was somewhat smaller in diameter than the main part, providing a step-like recess around the lower rim of the kettle. The projecting bottom fitted into the opening in the stove top, bringing the kettle closer to the fire. It also provides us with a recognition feature to distinguish kettles of the post-fireplace age (see Fig. 15).

The history of the cooking vessel has been summarized by Lifshey (1973). For many years after the coming of the cooking stove, pots and kettles were still made of cast iron. These were subject to rusting and corrosion, especially if used for acidic foods. The first major improvement occurred about 1873, when Jacob J. Vollwrath of Sheboygan, Wisconsin, introduced a process for coating iron vessels with a heat and acid resistant enamel. In 1892, stamped sheet-metal utensils appeared. During July, 1886, aluminum ware was introduced by the Pittsburgh Reduction Company, which later became the Aluminum Company of America.

One special fireplace utensil, the coffee roaster, had an interesting history in the stove era. At first the cylindrical container was mounted on some sort of housing, so as to fit over the opening in the stove top. Various improvements were made, as in the 1858

KEROSENE OIL STOVES.

1 Burner Game.
1 Burner Game, 4 inch Wick, Iron Reservoir.   List per doz...$17 00

No. 1. Single Gem.

No. 1 Single Gem has two 3   inch Wicks. List each........$2 80
No. 2   "   "   "   3½   "   "   " 3 30
No. 3   "   "   "   4   "   "   " 4 00

2 Burner Game.

List per doz
2 Burner Game, two 4 inch Wicks, Iron Reservoir...$36 00

No. 1 Double Gem.

No. 1—Double (see cut), four 3 inch Wicks.   List each.................$6 00
No. 5—   "   (same style, larger), four 4 inch Wicks.   List each 8 30

3 Burner Champion.
List per doz
3 Burner Champion, three 4 inch Wicks, Iron Reservoir......$54 00

The Volunteer.

This Stove has 4-inch wick, nickel trimmings, with mica on both sides.   The wick tube and rachet is hinged on, making it easy to re-wick and fill.   The base is heavy Japanned tin, neatly ornamented.

List Price, per dozen..................................$15 00
See page 133 for prices on ovens for above.

Fig. 31. Kerosene stoves, catalogue of H. Leonard &
Sons, Grand Rapids, Michigan, 1891.

Courtesy of The Henry Ford Museum,
Dearborn, Michigan.

patent[12] of C.J.C. Petersen of Davenport, Iowa, in which the container was provided with a heat damper, or in the patent[13] of the same year issued to Theodore Heermans, Mitchellville, Tennessee, in which internal vanes served to mix the coffee beans during rotation. Some of these stove-top roasters were spherical in form, as in the patent[14] of Samuel Tower, Grand Rapids, Michigan, 1858.

A radical departure in coffee roasters appeared in the patent[15] of Robert Brown, Ashtabula, Ohio, also in 1858. In this the container is in the form of a low, sheet-metal pot with a lid. Projecting through the center of the lid is a shaft, from which four paddles or scrapers extend on arms of different lengths within the pot. The shaft is to be turned through two bevel gears from a horizontal shaft with a handle. The container with its charge of beans would be placed on the open stove top and the handle turned. Each rotating blade swept a different circle, thus assuring good distribution of the roasting coffee, in spite of any irregularities that the heat might have caused in the roaster bottom.

Similar coffee roasters were made of cast iron. In those that survive, the indirect gear-drive has been dispensed with, and replaced by a handle attached to the upper end of the elongated rotating shaft. In the example shown (Fig. 32) there are only two internal paddles, one sweeping the inner portion of the circular bottom, the opposite one an outer path. The discomfort that might be caused to the operator by having to stand close to the stove was partly overcome by having a long shaft, which elevated the handle well above the source of heat.

The luxury of one generation is the hardship of the next. No cook of the mid-nineteenth century would willingly have gone back from cooking stove to fireplace. Most modern cooks, with their automated gas or electric stoves and microwave ovens, would feel greatly abused by a forced return to wood or coal as a fuel. But the memory of the kitchen stove, with its comforting warmth and appetizing aromas, includes few of the unpleasant associations. Bringing in the fuel, starting the fire, taking out the ashes, and cleaning the stove with a messy black polish, are almost forgotten. And the atavistic lure of cooking on an open fire finds fulfillment in the out-door barbecue.

a   b

Fig. 32. Stove-top coffee roaster: (a) closed; (b) open to show paddle. LSR Collection.

3 *Preparation of Food*

"Man cannot live by bread alone" but he cannot live without it either. By the end of the 18th century the standard of living in North American households had risen to a level that involved complex operations for the preparation of food. But most of this was still being done with simple tools and by hand. Meat was cut with a knife into pieces suitable for frying or broiling. Fish and fowl were slit open and cleaned. Vegetables were pared and sliced by hand. It was not until people began preparing food for preservation, to be cooked and eaten later, that the more elaborate techniques and complex devices appeared. Although salting and smoking were manual operations, the grinding of meat for sausages and the stuffing of it into the tubular "cases" could be done better with mechanical devices, which became more ingenious as the 19th century progressed. Chopping vegetables was too simple an operation to require more than a knife blade, but finer mincing for soups and stews could involve mechanical utensils. Cutting cabbage for sauerkraut was best done on some kind of shredding board.

Preparation of fruit was well suited to mechanization; fruit could be dried and stored, or preserved with added sugar in tight jars. In such tasks it was better to prepare large quantities at a time, and devices to speed up the process were highly desirable. Thus there was an early and widespread use of mechanical apple parers and corers, cherry pitters, and raisin seeders. For more immediate use there were miniature presses for squeezing out fruit juices.

Home-grown herbs when dried, could be crushed by hand, but the imported spices were either ground (pepper) or grated (nutmeg). The commonest kitchen grinder was that used for the roasted coffee beans, and coffee "mills" were almost as varied as apple parers, and probably more widely used.

Mechanical stirring devices came rather late, but by the 1860s the geared egg beater was available. Larger stirrers were used for making modest amounts of butter. The process of butter-making lent itself well to mechanization as a substitute for the tedious working of the dasher churn and butter paddle. For storage or sale, butter was shaped into sophisticated moulds.

Choppers

The manual chopping of meat and vegetables was commonly done in a hardwood or burl bowl, using a knife that could be pushed down from above. Such a knife looks like the Eskimo woman's *ooloo*, but was used with a chopping rather than a slicing motion. There were many variations on the basic design. The simplest was that in which the blade and handle were parallel but offset (Fig. 33). This would work best on a flat chopping board, as would any chopper with a straight edge, even with the handle above the blade. For use in a bowl a convex blade was more suitable (Fig. 34). There were various shapes of blade and attachments for the handle. Some choppers were home-made, others were factory-produced (Fig. 35). The latter included some with two parallel blades, spaced about an inch apart. Chopping knives of this sort were still being sold and used at the end of the 19th century. In 1893 a patent[1] was obtained by Nelson R. Streeter of Groton, N.Y., for a double-blade chopper in which the blades could be removed for sharpening (Fig. 36). Another chopper, patented[2] the same day by J.W. Allen of Richford, N.Y., had two blades set at right angles.

A complicated but ingenious mechanical chopper appeared in 1865, the invention of Le Roy S. Starrett of Newburyport. Massachusetts.[3] This must have been used widely, as many examples have survived (Fig. 37). At

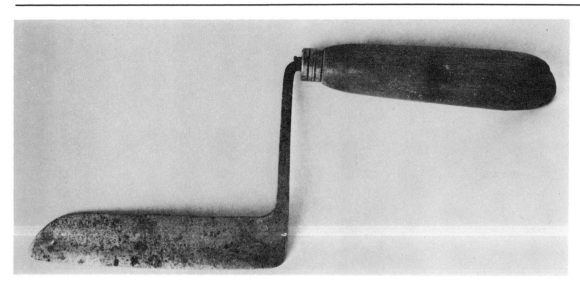

Fig. 33. Chopping knife, LSR Collection.

one end of the platform base is a cylindrical container for the food. In this there are one or two vertical cutting blades, mounted off-center at one end of a pivoted "walking-beam". The other end of the beam is coupled to a vertical reciprocating shaft, which is moved by an off-center attachment to a fly-wheel shaft. On the outside of the fly wheel is another off-center attachment, which provides motion to a long, diagonal shaft, and this acts as a pawl against a circular ratchet around the base of the food container.

Fig. 34. Chopping knife, Black Creek Pioneer Village, Toronto.

Fig. 35. Chopping knife, Black Creek Pioneer Village, Toronto.

Fig. 36. Chopping knife, Streeter patent, 1893. LSR Collection.

In use the fly wheel was turned by a handle and crank through two gears. This caused the blades to rise and fall rapidly within the container, while at the same time the container itself rotated, thus providing a uniform chopping of the meat or vegetables therein.

The following year (1866) H.W. Russell of Stoughton, Massachusetts, patented[4] a similar food chopper with a single chopping blade, and with the chopping and rotating action transmitted by gears. No example of this version has been recognized as yet.

Slicers

Slicing potatoes, onions, and cabbages in preparation for cooking was normally done with a knife on a board. For a large family or a community meal a shredding board was better (Fig. 38). This is long and narrow, and has an oblique slot near midlength along which a sharp steel blade is mounted. The arrangement is like that of a carpenter's plane, but in use the shredding board is held with the blade side up, and the vegetable to be sliced is pushed down the face of the board against the blade. The cut slices fall through the slot into a container. Usually the board was held at a slope, with the far end resting on a table, but some models had four legs, which could be folded for storage. Shredding devices based on this principle are still being made, but they are of plastic, and some have interchangeable blades of various shapes.

A common use of shredding boards was in the making of sauerkraut. Among the Pennsylvania Germans this fermented cabbage dish was made in large quantities, often on a community scale. For this kind of operation an extra large board was used, four feet or more in length. Convenience and safety were provided by use of a box-like holder, which slides in grooves on the sides of the board. The cabbage was placed in the box and held down by hand or with a block

Fig. 37. Food chopper, Starrett patent, 1865. Black Creek Pioneer Village, Toronto.

of wood, and the slicing motion was produced by pushing the box, not the cabbage.

For slicing fruit for drying or preserving, simple devices were used to make the operation quicker and easier. Apples were cut into quarters or eighths by means of a frame with sharp metal partitions extending from walls to center. The apple was either placed on a board and the sharp edges forced down through it, or it was pushed through by means of a block of wood. Some of these slicers had a tubular cutter at the center, which took out the core at the same time that the slices were being cut. Slicing and coring devices of this sort were incorporated in many mechanical apple parers.

For drying it was more desirable to slice the apple into wafers. Ingenious mechanical devices were made for this purpose. In one there is a fan-like arrangement of knife blades, which was swung across the apple in such a way as to cut off successive slices. Another has a set of fork-like arms, which by means of a lever can push an apple through a staggered set of horizontal blades (Fig. 39).

Fig. 38. Vegetable shredder, Black Creek Pioneer Village, Toronto.

Fig. 39. Apple slicer, Royal Ontario Museum, Toronto.

Meat Grinders

The preparation of ground meat for sausage filling and other purposes was originally done by manual chopping, but in 1859, John C. Perry of Kingston, Rhode Island, patented[5] a mechanical grinder that achieved popularity. It consists of a cylindrical iron chamber in which is a core that can be rotated by means of an external crank (Fig. 40). The core has spiral rows of short, square teeth, which mesh with straight rows of sharp teeth within the chamber. Meat was intro- duced into the chamber through a hopper, and the spiral arrangement of the core teeth carried it forward, forcing it between the sharp teeth, and pushing the chopped product through an opening at the end. For

a

b

Fig. 40. Meat grinder, Perry patent, 1859: (a) closed in operating position; (b) open to show mechanism. National Museum of Man, Ottawa.

cleaning, the upper half of the chamber wall is hinged, so that it can be swung back to expose the interior.

The Henry Ford Museum at Dearborn, Michigan, has two grinders built on the Perry design, but in these the chamber is of wood. Although it is suggested that these were made by "the man of the house" their sophisticated design would indicate, rather, that they are probably prototypes of the cast-iron version described in the patent.

On the same date as the Perry patent, Albert W. Hale of New Britain, Connecticut, obtained a patent[6] for a meat grinder which also consisted of a cast-iron chamber, but this was shaped like two incomplete cylinders joined together along the middle. Within this double-barreled chamber are two revolving cores, with sharp spiral ridges. Opposing these is a series of low, sharp ridges on the inner surface of the chamber. When meat was introduced through an opening in the lid of the chamber and the handle turned, the spiral ridges carried the meat forward, at the same time grinding it against the ridges on the chamber wall.

In the late 1800s a type of meat grinder appeared in which the spirally-ridged revolving core was used, but only to carry the meat forward from hopper to grinding mechanism. The earliest of these that I have found is the "Enterprise Meat Chopper" (Fig. 41), which is illustrated and described in the 1883 catalogue of the Enterprise Manu-facturing Company of Philadelphia. In this grinder the revolving core forced the meat through perforations in a stationary plate at the end of the case. Five different models are shown, the "family size" being clamped rather than screwed to the table. This grinder was advertised in the Sears, Roebuck Catalogue of 1897.

The meat grinder that has survived in various forms, and has been electrified for modern use, appeared in the patents[7] of 1897 and 1899 by Levi Tracy Snow of New Haven, Connecticut. The Snow grinder (Fig. 42) resembles the Enterprise grinder in the use of

Fig. 41. Meat grinder, Enterprise Mfg. Co., ca. 1883. LSR Collection.

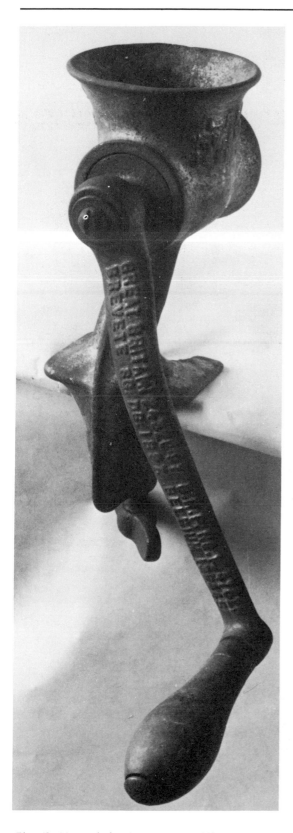

Fig. 42. Meat grinder, Snow patent, 1897. LSR Collection.

a revolving core to press the meat against the end plate, but the latter has relatively large openings. As the meat emerged through these it was further comminuted by a toothed wheel attached to the shaft of the revolving core. Provision was made for using four- or eight-toothed wheels for coarse or fine cutting. The example shown, while incomplete, bears the dates or numbers of the American, Canadian, British, French, and Belgian patents, and the inscription: L.F. & C. / NEW BRITAIN / CONN. U.S.A.

Many versions of the Snow grinder appeared in the 20th century. One of the earliest was that patented[8] by Henry Gustave Voight of New Britain, Connecticut, in 1901 and 1902 (Fig. 43). In this a sloping trough is provided along the lower part of the case, to catch dripping juice, and deliver it to the grinding end. Also, the case is in two parts, hinged so that the left half can be swung down for cleaning the interior, or secured in place for operation by a catch on the top of the case. In addition to the Canadian and American patent dates, the grinder bears the inscription: RUSSWIN / No. 1 and RUSSELL & IRWIN / MFG. CO. / NEW BRITAIN, / CONN. U.S.A.

Coffee Grinders

Grinding the roasted coffee beans before use was a daily household task for many housewives in the 19th century. This insured freshness. The common form of "coffee mill" in North America was of European origin, and consisted of a wooden box with the grinding mechanism set in the top (Fig. 44). The coffee beans were poured into the funnel-like hopper, at the bottom of which is a circular row of teeth. These work against a similar row on a rotary cutter, which turns on a vertical shaft connected to a crank. The pulverized coffee fell from the grinder into the box and was caught in a drawer, which could be withdrawn and emptied when the desired amount of coffee had been ground.

The wooden-box coffee grinder continued to be sold and used throughout the

a

b

Fig. 43. Meat grinder, Voight patent, 1901: (a) closed, in operating position; (b) open to show cutting mechanism. LSR Collection.

19th century. Minor changes were made: improvements in the grinding mechanism, covers added to the hoppers, metallic boxes substituted for those of wood. All-metal grinders appeared in the 1840s (Fig. 45). Some of these were intended to be fastened to the wall. A design that persisted until late in the century was patented[9] in 1845 by Beriah Smith of Washington, N.Y. (Fig. 46). In this the hopper was triangular in outline, and fed into a flat, drum-shaped grinding chamber. The ground coffee emerged through an opening in the bottom and was caught in a jar or other receptacle. Other wall-mounted coffee grinders were provided with a clamp to secure a jar under the outlet.

The firm most closely associated with coffee grinders was the Enterprise Manufacturing Company of Philadelphia. Sold under the name of American Coffee, Spice and Drug Mill, they were mostly intended for use by grocers and coffee dealers. Some of them were relatively enormous in size. With their large fly wheels and bright colors, they were the most conspicuous feature of the old-time general store. The Enterprise grinders were based mainly on the patents[10]

of John G. Baker of Philadelphia. The distinctive feature of the Baker grinder is the three-part construction of the cast-iron case. This consists of an upper, vase-shaped hopper, with or without lid, a spherical grinding chamber, and a box-shaped receptacle at the base. The grinding chamber can be opened by swinging back on a hinge the upper part of the case. The grinding mechanism consists of vertical milling discs driven directly by a horizontal shaft connected to a crank or a fly wheel. Along with the large grinders for commercial use, the Enterprise line included their No. 1 (Fig. 47), a small model without fly wheel, for use in homes.

Domestic coffee grinders continued to be sold and used until well into the 20th century. By this time, however, most people were buying their coffee already ground at the store. The introduction of packaged coffee did away for a time with the coffee grinder in store and home, but in modern times they have reappeared in electrically driven form at the "supermarket", so that customers can buy the packaged beans and grind them to a desired fineness. Small electric grinders for

a   b

*Fig. 44. Coffee grinder: (a) operating position;
(b) hopper and drawer open. LSR Collection.*

Fig. 45. Various coffee grinders, National Museum of Man, Ottawa.

Fig. 46. Wall-mounted coffee grinder, Swift patents, 1845 and 1859. LSR Collection.

home use are now available for those who wish to have freshly ground coffee each morning.

Beaters

Eggs for omelets or cakes have to be beaten vigorously to a uniform consistency. Some sauces also require strenuous stirring. Originally this was done with a spoon or a fork in a bowl. Simple hand beaters of wire loops on a handle were also used. The introduction of metallic gears early in the 19th century made the design of mechanical egg beaters practical. Most of these consisted of a main gear wheel with a handle, revolving in a vertical plane, and transmitting motion to a small horizontal gear attached in such a way as to cause one or more wires or metal strips to revolve rapidly when the handle was turned. A number of patents for beaters of this sort were issued in the late 1850s and the 1860s. The earliest to achieve much popularity was the invention[11] of J.F. and E.P. Monroe of New York, N.Y., in 1859. This has ten rotating wires, curved in below to join a

American Coffee, Spice and Drug Mill,
No. 1.
With Iron Hopper, holding 4 ounces Coffee.

SHOWING N° I MILL CLOSED.

SHOWING N° I. MILL OPEN.

The above cuts represent our smallest Counter Mill, both closed and open, and illustrate the simple principle of operating our Mills, and the easy mode of opening them. It stands 12½ inches high, weighs 8 pounds, grinds 6 ounces of Coffee per minute, and is regulated either coarse or fine by a thumb screw on the side. It is adapted to family use and prescription counters.

PRICE, ... $2.00.

American Coffee, Spice and Drug Mill,
No. 2.   No. 2½.

Our Nos. 2 and 2½ Mills are alike, excepting as to dome, and will grind 6 ounces of coffee per minute. They are very desirable for prescription counters and family use.

Iron Hopper; stands 10½ inches high, and weighs 10 pounds.

PRICE, $3.00.

Nickel-plated dome; stands 15 inches high, and weighs 10 pounds.

PRICE, $4.00.

Extra Grinders, for Nos. 1, 2, 2½, 3, 4, ...	per pair,	$ .75
" " " 5, 6, 7, 8, ...	"	1.00
" " " 9 to 18, ...	"	1.50
" " " 19 and 20, ...	"	3.00

Grinders Warranted equal to Steel.

Fig. 47. Enterprise coffee grinders, Enterprise Mfg. Co. catalogue, 1883. Pennsylvania Historical Society, Philadelphia.

vertical shaft. The shaft provided good stability and control. The Monroe beater was advertised in the Dover Stamping Co. catalogue of 1869 as being "too well known to the public to need our recommendation". In 1874 the Monroes improved their beater and assigned the patent to the Dover Stamping Co.

A beater with metal strips instead of wires was patented[12] in 1863 by Timothy Earle of Smithfield, Rhode Island. In this the strip is in the form of a loop, attached at its lower end to a central shaft. The stirring surface is increased by having two or three additional strips attached to the inside of the main loop. In his patent Earle shows a straight bar with gear teeth, which was pushed back and forth to impact motion to the shaft. But the version pictured in the Dover catalogue of 1869 shows the conventional gear wheel with handle.

The Dover Stamping Company produced their own version of a beater in the early 1890s (Fig. 48), the patented invention[13] of E.H. Whitney and J.L. Kirby of Cambridge, Massachusetts, 1891. This has two strip loops, straight above, circular below, ingeniously geared to rotate in opposite directions at 90° to each other. This principle was incorporated into other beaters, and persists today in both hand-operated and electrically driven versions.

A wire stirrer of unusual design was incorporated in the beater patented[14] in 1886 by George H. Thomas of Chicopee Falls, Massachusetts. In this there is a central shaft, at the lower end of which is attached a conically coiled spring. According to Franklin (p. 83), this beater was advertised in the Montgomery Ward catalogue of 1895.

Another beater using wire loops was patented[15] by Edwin Baltzley of Washington, D.C., in 1885, and marketed by the Keystone Manufacturing Company of Philadelphia (Fig. 49). In this there is a short shaft terminating below in a "beater head", which is driven by gears from the main wheel. Attached to this head, but free to swing independently, are some seven to nine wire loops. When the beater is operated rapidly, these loops swing out centrifugally to a wide angle. Such a beater must have been very

Fig. 48. Eggbeater, Whitney and Kirby patent, 1891; Dover Stamping Co. LSR Collection.

effective in light fluids, such as milk, but would not have worked well in heavier mixtures, such as sauces, and the wire loops look as if they could be easily damaged. Baltzley called his device a "culinary beater", so he must have intended it for a variety of substances. This beater was advertised in glowing terms in the 1888 catalogue of H. Leonard and Sons of Grand Rapids, Michigan. It is shown with both wall and table mounts, while examples existing today have a clamp to fit the top of a jar.

Parers

No domestic appliance typifies more graphically the 19th-century mechanization of the kitchen than the apple parer. The peeling of fruit and vegetables by hand was a tedious process; it was usually done with a small blade ("paring-knife"), which was grasped with the fingers while the thumb pressed against the object to be peeled. Inevitably the ball of the thumb acquired a few nicks or slits. A safer instrument was a knife with a wire guard in front of the edge, with a space for the peel to emerge (Fig. 50). Depth of paring was more uniform and less wasteful. A hand parer and corer that achieved long-term popularity was patented[16] in 1877 by W.E. Brock of New York, N.Y. This was a blade in the shape of a half-cylinder, with a longitudinal slot having one or both edges sharpened. With this a thin peel could be stripped off with no danger to the fingers. One end of the blade was sharpened and pointed, making it useful for coring apples or prying the eyes out of potatoes. Parers of this sort are still being made and sold.

Where orchards were extensive and productive, the large-scale preparation of the fruit for drying or for making "apple butter" became a community activity, carried out at a "paring bee", an event especially popular with young people as the boys and girls worked together. There was a competitive spirit on these occasions and some sort of mechanization was advantageous. So the first mechanical apple parers appeared, in

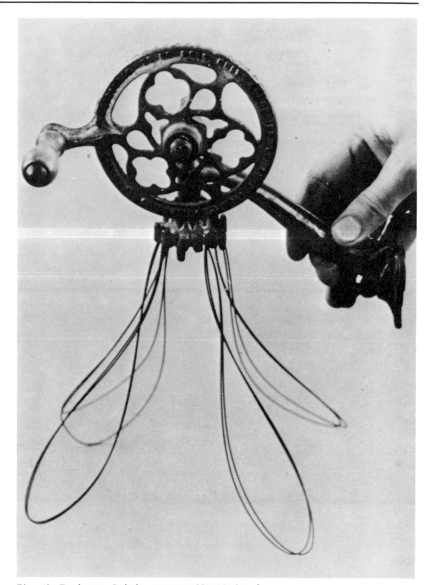

Fig. 49. Eggbeater, Baltzley patent, 1885. National Museum of Man, Ottawa.

simplest form, a two-tined fork mounted on an axle with a hand crank at the other end. To increase the speed of rotation a pulley drive was introduced, probably copied from the spindle mechanism of the spinning wheel. The crank turned a large pulley, from which a loop of cord drove a small pulley on the shaft of the apple holder. Whether the drive was direct or indirect, the actual paring was done by holding a sharp knife-edge against the rotating fruit.

It is said that there was keen competition among the young men at the paring bees not only to peel the largest number of apples, but

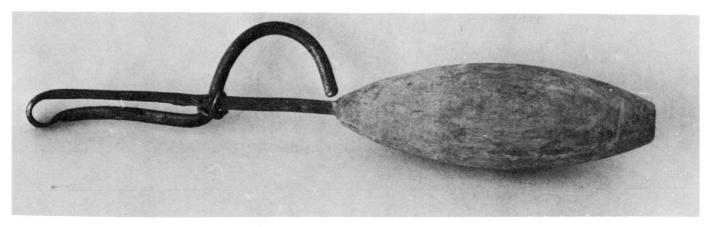

Fig. 50. Paring knife, LSR Collection.

Fig. 51. Wooden apple parer with pulley drive, LSR Collection.

also to have the most ingenious and impressive parer. This led to the devising of more sophisticated parers. A second set of pulley wheels was incorporated to give faster rotation (Fig. 51). Or instead of pulleys, a gear drive might be used. This usually took the form of a wooden disc with a crank handle and a ring of pegs projecting from near the rim, and arranged to mesh with a small gear wheel on the shaft of the apple holder.

The cutting blade soon progressed beyond the simple knife. As the surface to be peeled was convex, a short blade was as effective as a long one. In an arrangement similar to the modern safety razor the blade was mounted transversely on a wooden handle, in some examples shaped to guide the blade on the rotating fruit. The next step was to mount the knife on a jointed support, so that it required only a moderate amount of manual guidance. From this it was only a step to the parer in which the movement of the blade was controlled by the mechanism, but this had to wait for the introduction of metal gears.

Many wooden apple parers were of elegant as well as ingenious construction, reflecting the competition to produce the most admirable machine. Some makers signed and dated their creations (Fig. 52). Securing the parer was usually done by screwing or clamping it to a table top. Often, however, the device was mounted at one end of a long board, the other end of which could be placed on a chair or stool and sat upon by the operator. Some parers were attached to a

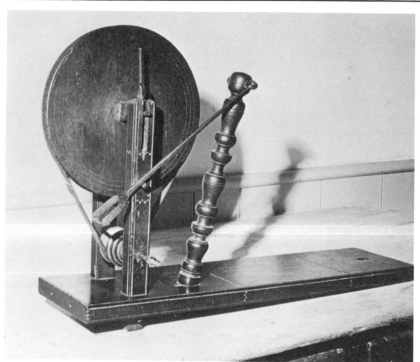

*Fig. 52. Wooden apple parer, David Byer, 1843:
(a) general view; (b) inscription on base.
Black Creek Pioneer Village, Toronto.*

three-legged bench, like that used by leather workers.

With the potential for ingenious inventions so inherent in the mechanical apple parer, it was not long before they began to appear in formal letters patent. The earliest of these[17] was issued to Moses Coates of Chester County, Pa., in 1803. The text of this patent is preserved in the U.S. National Archives, but without illustration. However, a perspective drawing of the device was published in the American edition of Anthony Willich's "Domestic Encyclopedia", edited by J. Mease, 1804. This was reproduced in the "American Artists Manual" by James Cutbush, 1814, and in Franklin, 1976 (p. 3). From these sources, including the patent, I prepared the accompanying drawing (Fig. 53). The base is a simple board, at one end of which two uprights support a horizontal shaft. One end of this shaft has a crank, the other a three-tined fork. The paring knife is mounted in a wooden block, like a spoke shave, which is supported by two long, flexible strips of spring metal. The other ends of these strips are attached to a kind of rocking beam, which is broadly V-shaped. In use, the operator impaled the apple on the fork. He turned the crank with the right hand while guiding the knife block around the surface of the apple with the left hand. According to Dr. Mease, the device allowed the apples to be pared with great rapidity.

In 1809, S. Crittenden of Guilford, Maine, obtained a patent[18] for a combined parer and corer, but this patent was lost in the 1836 fire. R.W. Mitchell, of Springfield, Ohio, was issued a patent[19] in 1838 for a combined parer, slicer, and corer. The apple was carried on a horizontal shaft, as in the Coates parer. The paring blade was mounted on a universal joint, and held against the apple by hand. After paring, the impaled apple was pushed against four radial blades and a cylindrical cutter mounted at the end of the frame. The apple quarters fell out through a chute and the core was expelled at the end of the cutter. This device was only a combination of the wooden apple parer and the slicer-corer, but it differed from most in that the rotary shaft was without pulleys or gears and was longitudinal to the frame, not transverse. Although no examples of the Mitchell parer seem to have survived, it was directly ancestral to one form of metallic parer.

Apple parers of metal appeared in the 1840s. Metallic gears lent themselves to many elaborations not possible with pulleys or wooden gears. In the 1850s there was a flood of patents for such devices. Now at last the paring knife became fully automatic, moving across the rotating apple and conforming to its shape. Metal apple parers are of two types, which may be called the screw parer and the gear parer. The former is simpler and might

be presumed to be earlier, but the gear type was derived directly from the more advanced wooden parers.

An early type of screw parer is shown in Fig. 54. It bears a paper label of which the only decipherable part reads "Bay State Apple". The shaft with the two-tined apple fork is turned by a crank wheel with inside teeth. This kind of drive is common in apple parers, as it rotates the apple in the same direction that the crank is turned. The shaft is coarsely threaded, more like a worm than a screw. The cutting mechanism is mounted to slide on a longitudinal rod near the base of the device. It has a vertical arm at the near end, the tip of which engages the thread of the shaft. At the other end of the cutter base is a spring-loaded knife holder. As the shaft with its apple was turned clockwise (as seen from the near end), the threaded shaft, through the arm and cutter base, drew the blade towards the operator, passing over and conforming to the shape of the apple by means of a swivel joint and the pressure of the spring. To free the apple for removal one pulled the cutter mechanism forward and pushed it to a disengaged position on the left. This parer and a long line like it appear to have been

Fig. 53. Apple parer, Coates patent, 1803; drawing by LSR, based on the illustration in Franklin, 1976, p. 3, and the original description.

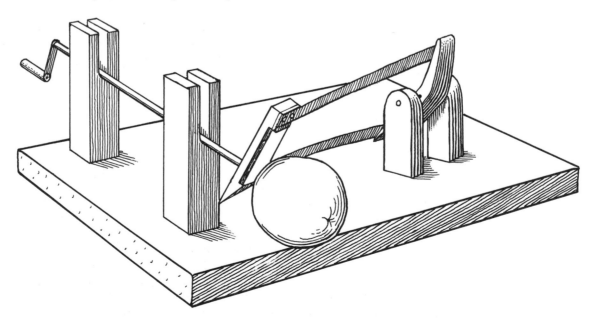

Fig. 54. "Bay State" apple parer, based on the Carter patent of 1849, National Museum of Man, Ottawa.

based on the patent[20] of Charles P. Carter of Ware, Mass., 1849, which is the earliest that I have found in which the movement of the paring knife is controlled by a worm or screw on the horizontal shaft. More sophisticated versions were patented[21] by Carter in 1856. In these the apple was cored as well as peeled, and could be sliced spirally.

The best-known inventor of screw-type parers was David H. Whittemore of Worcester, Mass. In the Worcester City Directory of 1851 he is listed as "machinist" and in the 1857 Directory as a manufacturer of paring machines, etc. It was in 1857 that he obtained his first two patents[22] for apple parers (Fig. 55). These were based on the Carter parer but with certain innovations, the more important being that the cutting blade was narrowly curved, and the rod on which the paring and slicing knives moved was bent inward at its far end, to allow the blades to begin cutting closer to the end of the apple. A gear-type parer was patented[23] by Whittemore in 1866. In this the motion of the knife was controlled by cams on the side of the secondary wheel. This was advertised in 1869 under the name of Union Apple-Paring Machine, perhaps a patriotic reference to the recent war.

Whittemore returned to the screw-type parer in his patent[24] of 1869. Unlike his 1857 parers, this one has a gear drive, the master gear having internal teeth. Through small, separate gears this operates both the screw and the fork shaft. In the example seen by me the table clamp is at an angle to the vertical axis of the parer, so that the crank does not clear the table edge if clamped in the usual way. In 1871 Whittemore obtained reissues of his 1857 patents. The last entry for him in the Worcester City Directory is for 1859, but he was active subsequently; he obtained a patent for a gear-type parer in 1881, and for screw-type parers in 1881, 1882, and 1883.[25]

Parers with metal gears appeared in the 1850s and for the remainder of the century were patented and manufactured in great variety. An early version was that of J.D. Browne of Cincinnati, Ohio, patented[26] in 1856. In this (Fig. 56) a large, hand-turned gear wheel drives a small upper gear on the shaft that bears the prongs for the apple. Another small gear on the axis of the drive

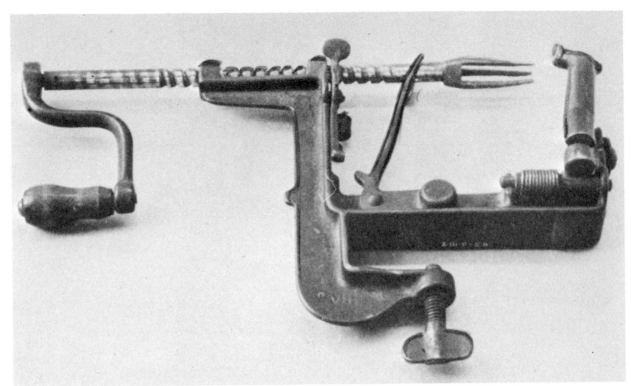

*Fig. 55. Apple parer, Whittemore patent, 1857,
National Museum of Man, Ottawa.*

gear rotates a horizontal gear, to which is attached an arm. This arm moves the shaft that bears the cutting blade; the shaft has a characteristic shape, vertical above, coiled spirally below to provide spring pressure. The arrangement of gear and arm is such as to cause the shaft and knife to move through a half-circle, at the end of which it is released to swing back to the starting position. The Browne parer was made by the Scott Mfg. Co. of Baltimore, Md., and a number of examples have survived.

Of the many inventors who obtained patents for gear-type parers in the later 1800s, a few were conspicuous because of the number of patents issued to them and because of the numerous examples of their inventions that have survived. In 1856 Horatio Keyes of Leominster, Mass., obtained a patent[27] for a relatively simple parer. In this a large vertical gear wheel with handle drives a smaller upper gear attached to the apple-prong shaft. The axle of the drive gear terminates in a small bevel gear, which meshes with a large horizontal bevel gear, to

which is attached by a pivot the arm of the paring blade. The lower end of this arm engages the inner edge of a fixed template cut in such a shape as to cause the arm and its blade to swing through a nearly circular path around the apple, then spring away and return to its starting position. In 1861 S.S. Hersey of Farmington, Maine, patented[28] a gear-type parer in which a spur on the main gear causes the spring-loaded knife arm to fly back to the start on completion of the paring.

Perhaps the most frequently encountered name of an inventor of apple parers is that of Frederick W. Hudson. He was a resident of Leominster, Mass. most of his life. At first he worked for the firm of Lockey & Howland. W. M. Howland himself patented[29] a gear-type apple parer in 1864. Eventually Hudson left to set up the Hudson Parer Company on his own. He was joined by his son, C. E. Hudson, who took over the company in 1881 on his father's retirement. It was said in 1888 that the Hudson Parer Co. produced about fifty thousand machines annually.

The earliest of the Hudson parer

Fig. 56. Apple parer, Browne patent, 1856. The Henry Ford Museum, Dearborn, Michigan.

Photograph courtesy of The Henry Ford Museum.

patents,[30] dated 1862, involved a special gear drive to the apple holder so that it not only rotated on its axis, but also revolved in a circle relative to the paring knife. This was said to permit the parings to fall free of the mechanism. The same object was achieved differently in Hudson's patent[31] of 1872, in which the gear wheel that actuated the cutter arm was mounted vertically, well clear of the apple and the blade. In his patent[32] of 1874 he added a device of gears and levers to push the apple off the fork on completion of paring. A simplification of the gear-type parer appeared in his patent[33] of 1882, in which the "gear table", i.e., the geared disc that actuates the paring arm, was driven directly by a small gear attached to the main gear through a conical frame. The second Hudson patent[34] of 1882 is for a screw-type parer in which the knives were borne on swinging arms, which through a cam were caused to swing clear of the fork to permit replacing the apple.

Another productive inventor of parers was A. G. Batchelder of Lowell, Mass. In 1869 he patented[35] a gear-type parer in which a cam-operated lever pushed the apple off the fork on completion of paring. His patent[36] of 1870 was for a reciprocating-gear parer, with an ejector. In 1872 he obtained two patents[37] for improvements on the rotary gear-type parer.

A different principle of geared apple parers appeared first in the 1853 patent[38] of William H. Lazelle of New York, N.Y. In this the basic part is a semicircular horizontal rack, at the centre of which a frame ("Lever") is pivoted. Near the other end of the frame is a small pinion wheel which meshes with the rack, and is axially attached to a larger gear outside of the rack. This meshes with a pinion which drives a shaft in the upper part of the frame, terminating in a fork for the apple. In use, the parer was clamped to a table top or held in the hand. With the apple in position, the frame with its gears was swung back and forth in an arc by means of a handle, causing the apple to revolve. A spring-loaded arm mounted on the rack pressed a knife blade against the apple, cutting and removing the peel. This type of parer was advertised in 1867 under the name of Lightning Apple Parer (Fig. 57).

The parer to end all parers appeared in the patent[39] issued in 1889 to Samuel Lyon of Pultneyville, N.Y. It is a relatively large

Fig. 57. Apple parer, Lazelle patent, 1853. National Museum of Man, Ottawa.

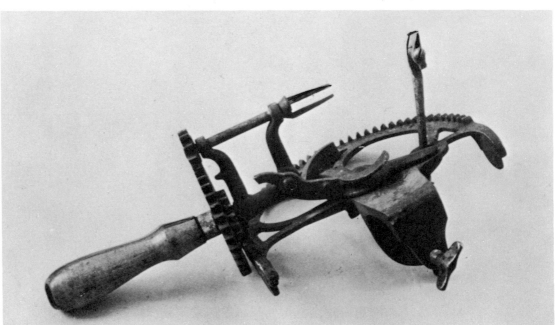

machine (Fig. 58) with the main gear-wheel with handle at one end. The shaft of the wheel terminates in a bevel gear, which turns a disc from which a hinged arm is suspended, bearing the cutter. The shaft also drives through a pinion a large gear wheel on the side of the frame, and this wheel, by means of a wrist-pin and a slotted lever, causes a

Fig. 58. Apple parer, Lyon patent, 1889: (a) front view; (b) rear view. National Museum of Man, Ottawa.

a

b

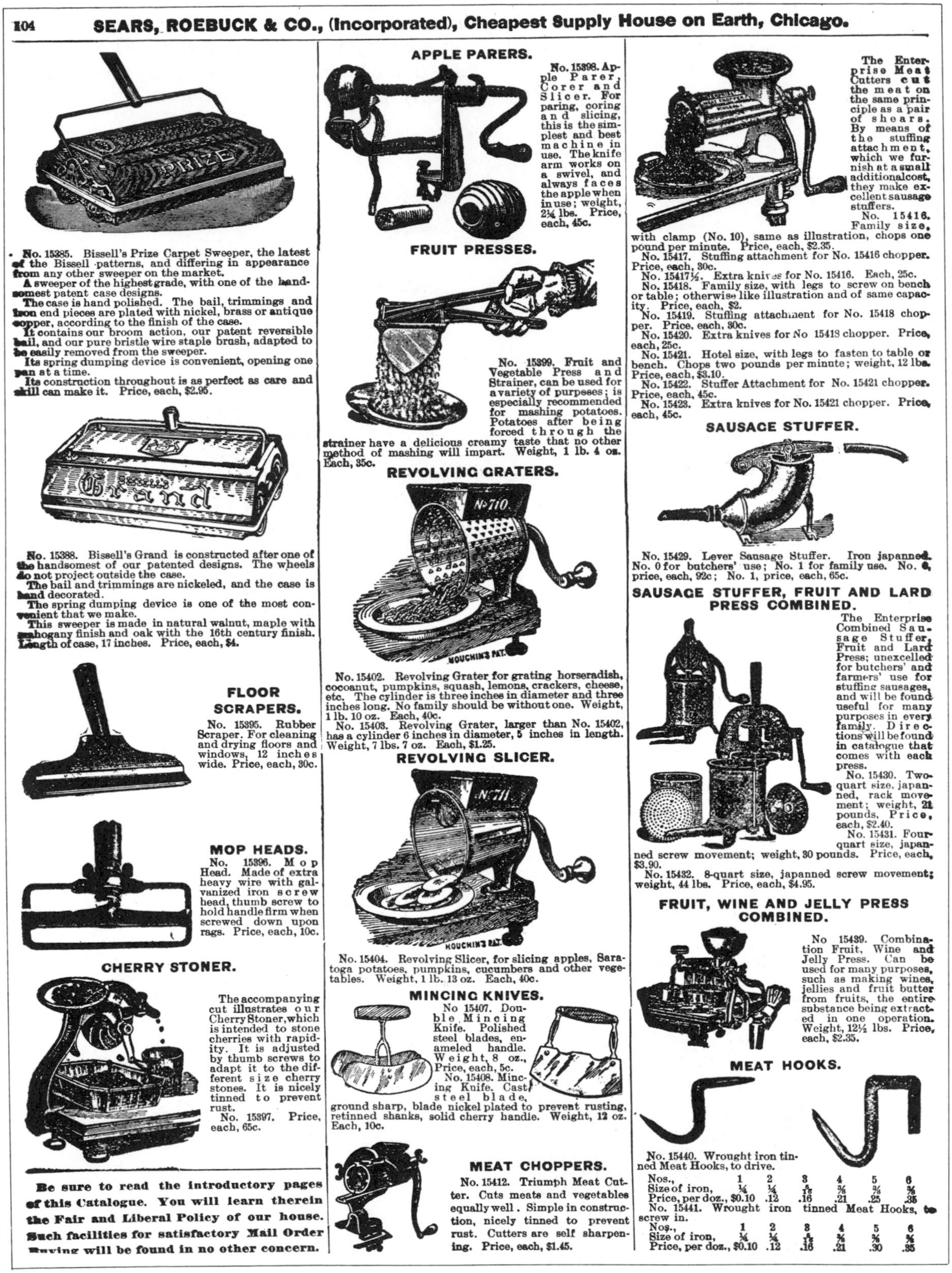

104 **SEARS, ROEBUCK & CO., (Incorporated), Cheapest Supply House on Earth, Chicago.**

No. 15385. Bissell's Prize Carpet Sweeper, the latest of the Bissell patterns, and differing in appearance from any other sweeper on the market.

A sweeper of the highest grade, with one of the handsomest patent case designs.

The case is hand polished. The bail, trimmings and iron end pieces are plated with nickel, brass or antique copper, according to the finish of the case.

It contains our broom action, our patent reversible bail, and our pure bristle wire staple brush, adapted to be easily removed from the sweeper.

Its spring dumping device is convenient, opening one pan at a time.

Its construction throughout is as perfect as care and skill can make it. Price, each, $2.95.

No. 15388. Bissell's Grand is constructed after one of the handsomest of our patented designs. The wheels do not project outside the case.

The bail and trimmings are nickeled, and the case is hand decorated.

The spring dumping device is one of the most convenient that we make.

This sweeper is made in natural walnut, maple with mahogany finish and oak with the 16th century finish. Length of case, 17 inches. Price, each, $4.

FLOOR SCRAPERS.

No. 15395. Rubber Scraper. For cleaning and drying floors and windows, 12 inches wide. Price, each, 30c.

MOP HEADS.

No. 15396. Mop Head. Made of extra heavy wire with galvanized iron screw head, thumb screw to hold handle firm when screwed down upon rags. Price, each, 10c.

CHERRY STONER.

The accompanying cut illustrates our Cherry Stoner, which is intended to stone cherries with rapidity. It is adjusted by thumb screws to adapt it to the different size cherry stones. It is nicely tinned to prevent rust.

No. 15397. Price, each, 65c.

Be sure to read the introductory pages of this Catalogue. You will learn therein the Fair and Liberal Policy of our house. Such facilities for satisfactory Mail Order Buying will be found in no other concern.

APPLE PARERS.

No. 15398. Apple Parer, Corer and Slicer. For paring, coring and slicing, this is the simplest and best machine in use. The knife arm works on a swivel, and always faces the apple when in use; weight, 2¼ lbs. Price, each, 45c.

FRUIT PRESSES.

No. 15399. Fruit and Vegetable Press and Strainer, can be used for a variety of purposes; is especially recommended for mashing potatoes. Potatoes after being forced through the strainer have a delicious creamy taste that no other method of mashing will impart. Weight, 1 lb. 4 oz. Each, 35c.

REVOLVING GRATERS.

No. 15402. Revolving Grater for grating horseradish, cocoanut, pumpkins, squash, lemons, crackers, cheese, etc. The cylinder is three inches in diameter and three inches long. No family should be without one. Weight, 1 lb. 10 oz. Each, 40c.

No. 15403. Revolving Grater, larger than No. 15402, has a cylinder 6 inches in diameter, 5 inches in length. Weight, 7 lbs. 7 oz. Each, $1.25.

REVOLVING SLICER.

No. 15404. Revolving Slicer, for slicing apples, Saratoga potatoes, pumpkins, cucumbers and other vegetables. Weight, 1 lb. 13 oz. Each, 40c.

MINCING KNIVES.

No 15407. Double Mincing Knife. Polished steel blades, enameled handle. Weight, 8 oz., Price, each, 5c.

No. 15408. Mincing Knife. Cast steel blade, ground sharp, blade nickel plated to prevent rusting, retinned shanks, solid cherry handle. Weight, 12 oz. Each, 10c.

MEAT CHOPPERS.

No. 15412. Triumph Meat Cutter. Cuts meats and vegetables equally well. Simple in construction, nicely tinned to prevent rust. Cutters are self sharpening. Price, each, $1.45.

The Enterprise Meat Cutters cut the meat on the same principle as a pair of shears. By means of the stuffing attachment, which we furnish at a small additional cost, they make excellent sausage stuffers.

No. 15416. Family size, with clamp (No. 10), same as illustration, chops one pound per minute. Price, each, $2.35.

No. 15417. Stuffing attachment for No. 15416 chopper. Price, each, 30c.

No. 15417½. Extra knives for No. 15416. Each, 25c.

No. 15418. Family size, with legs to screw on bench or table; otherwise like illustration and of same capacity. Price, each, $2.

No. 15419. Stuffing attachment for No. 15418 chopper. Price, each, 30c.

No. 15420. Extra knives for No 15418 chopper. Price, each, 25c.

No. 15421. Hotel size, with legs to fasten to table or bench. Chops two pounds per minute; weight, 12 lbs. Price, each, $3.10.

No. 15422. Stuffer Attachment for No. 15421 chopper. Price, each, 45c.

No. 15423. Extra knives for No. 15421 chopper. Price, each, 45c.

SAUSAGE STUFFER.

No. 15429. Lever Sausage Stuffer. Iron japanned. No. 0 for butchers' use; No. 1 for family use. No. 0, price, each, 92c; No. 1, price, each, 65c.

SAUSAGE STUFFER, FRUIT AND LARD PRESS COMBINED.

The Enterprise Combined Sausage Stuffer, Fruit and Lard Press; unexcelled for butchers' and farmers' use for stuffing sausages, and will be found useful for many purposes in every family. Directions will be found in catalogue that comes with each press.

No. 15430. Two-quart size, japanned, rack movement; weight, 21 pounds. Price, each, $2.40.

No. 15431. Four-quart size, japanned screw movement; weight, 30 pounds. Price, each, $3.90.

No. 15432. 8-quart size, japanned screw movement; weight, 44 lbs. Price, each, $4.95.

FRUIT, WINE AND JELLY PRESS COMBINED.

No 15439. Combination Fruit, Wine and Jelly Press. Can be used for many purposes, such as making wines, jellies and fruit butter from fruits, the entire substance being extracted in one operation. Weight, 12½ lbs. Price, each, $2.35.

MEAT HOOKS.

No. 15440. Wrought iron tinned Meat Hooks, to drive.

Nos.,	1	2	3	4	5	6
Size of iron,	¼	¼	5/16	⅜	⅜	⅜
Price, per doz.,	$0.10	.12	.16	.21	.25	.35

No. 15441. Wrought iron tinned Meat Hooks, to screw in.

Nos.,	1	2	3	4	5	6
Size of iron,	¼	¼	5/16	⅜	⅜	⅜
Price, per doz.,	$0.10	.12	.16	.21	.30	.35

Fig. 59. Apple parers, meat choppers, and presses, Sears, Roebuck and Co. catalogue, 1896.

Reproduction courtesy Sears, Roebuck and Co.

cutting tube to move against the apple, core it, and remove it on completion of the paring. The Lyon parer seems to be a very large and complicated machine for paring and coring one apple at a time, but from experience with it I can state that it works very well. It must have had some popularity, as numerous examples have survived. One in the National Museums of Canada is in the original packing box with the original lubricant still present. In addition to North American collections, there are two good examples in the Birdwood Museum of Technology and Applied Science at Birdwood, South Australia, one of which has been modified to hold two apples.

Widespread availability and excellent performance made the metal apple parer a common household article. The screw type is shown in the Sears, Roebuck and Co. catalogue for 1896 (Fig. 59). The mechanical apple parer largely eliminated the paring bee. One person could pare the same quantity of apples in less time than the community group could do using the old methods, and the results were more thorough and cleaner. But an interesting social tradition had been lost.

For paring other fruits, as well as vegetables, the ordinary apple parer was not completely successful. Peaches, with their more tender skins and their large stones, required special treatment. In the parer patented[40] in 1859 by A. Hermans of Henderson, Texas, the peach was held in a fork with elastic tines, and made to revolve against a fixed knife. The paring device of M. Smith of New Haven, Conn., patented[41] in 1860, had two forks, one at each end of the peach, to clasp the stone. The blade was fixed, and the peach-bearing mechanism travelled on a concave rail as it revolved.

The paring of potatoes presents a special problem; in addition to the irregular shape, there are numerous "eyes" that have to be removed. By substituting a narrow, concave blade for the usual flat knife, a nearly complete paring could be accomplished with the screw-type parer (Fig. 60). Even with this, however, some manual trimming was necessary. Special knives were devised for paring potatoes by hand, such as that patented[42] in 1860 by C. Digeton of

Fig. 60. Vegetable parer, "Triumph", LSR Collection.

Philadelphia, in which the angle of the blade was adjustable. Another approach to potato paring was to remove the skin with a kind of grater. W. H. Williams of Canton, Ohio, obtained a patent[43] in 1870 for such a parer. It consisted of a large, fixed cylinder having numerous projections on the inner surface, forming the grater. In the center was a conical core, also with sharp projections, but these were perforated, and opened into a series of spiral grooves inside the core. Potatoes were placed in the space between core and cylinder, and the core rotated by means of a vertical shaft and crank. The two sets of projections would strip off the skin, and the parings were supposed to work their way out through the perforated teeth and the inner grooves of the core. The pared potatoes were removed through a sliding door on the side of the cylinder.

Seed Removers

"Can she make a cherry pie, Billy Boy, Billy Boy?" asked the old song, attesting to the popularity of that delicious pastry. Cherry trees were planted at an early stage in colonial

Fig. 61. Cherry stoner, Buckwalter patent, 1863. U.S. patent drawing.

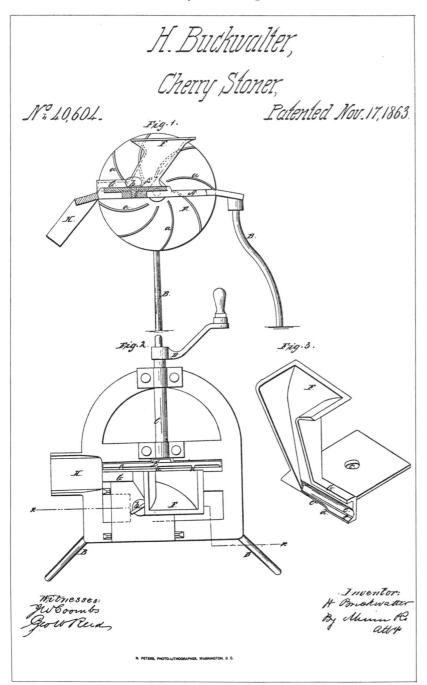

history, and they produced abundant fruit, which was used not only in the fresh form for pies, but also as a preserve for future pie fillings or desserts. In either case it was desirable, although not always the practice, to remove the cherry stones before cooking the fruit. By hand this was a tedious job, and in the 1860s, ingenious devices for the purpose were being patented and manufactured. The first to achieve popularity was the invention of Henry Buckwalter of Kimberton, Pennsylvania, patented[44] in 1863. It consisted of a vertically mounted disc of cast iron, having on one side a set of spirally curved ridges (Fig. 61). The disc was rotated by means of a crank. Cherries fed into the machine through a hopper were squeezed by the ridges of the rotating disc against a projecting shoulder of the frame. This forced out the stones, which fell through a chute on the end of the machine. The cherry pulp dropped onto a dish placed below, within the three legs of the device.

Three years later William Weaver of Phoenixville, Pennsylvania, patented[45] a modification of the Buckwalter stoner, in which the rotating disc had spiral ridges on both sides, and was partly enclosed by the hopper (Fig. 62). The machine was designed to be set up over the mouth of a jar to catch the pulp, and the stones were expelled into a dish on one side. Cherry stoners of the Buckwalter-Weaver type, but modified to clamp on the edge of a table, were advertised in the Sears, Roebuck and Company catalogue of 1897.

In the cherry stoner patented[46] in 1867 by George Geer of Galesburg, Illinois, the stones were punched rather than squeezed out (Fig. 63). The basic part of the Geer stoner is the pair of curved plungers, hinged at the base and attached to a handle so that they can be swung forward or back. In the forward position the ends of the plungers enter two perforated depressions in the near end of a rectangular, sloping trough, the floor of which has two channels leading to the two depressions. In operation the stoner was clamped to a table edge. Cherries were placed in the trough and by gravity rolled down the channels into the depressions. The plungers were then swung forward and downward;

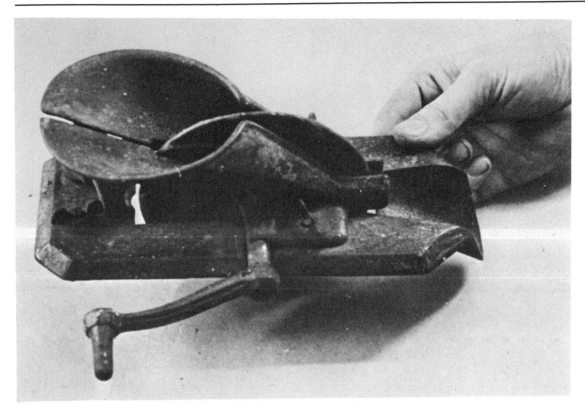

Fig. 62. Cherry stoner, Weaver patent, 1866. National
Museum of Man, Ottawa.

Fig. 63. Cherry stoner, Geer patent, 1867. National
Museum of Man, Ottawa.

by a slotted partition through which the plungers passed. The freed cherries fell into a sloping trough below the partition and rolled off into a dish placed at the side. In his original patent Geer stated that the stoned cherries would be caught in a bowl held on the operator's lap. The sloping trough, however, would drop the cherries to the side, rather than the front.

The punching type of cherry stoner reappeared in somewhat different form in the device patented[47] in 1870 by John N. Webster of Peoria, Illinois. The original patent shows a pair of plungers in parallel, but existing examples have only one plunger (Fig. 64). This is straight, and spring-loaded, so as normally to be in the up position. In operation it was pushed down manually so that the end, with spread points, entered a circular opening in the near end of an oval trough. When clamped to a table top the device sat on a slant, so that the cherries rolled down one by one to fit into the depression around the hole. The actual punching was the same as in the Geer stoner; the stones were pushed through a rubber washer in the hole, and the cherry lifted on the return stroke of the plunger and scraped off by a semi-circular bar joining the supports of the plunger. Later examples of the Webster stoner were modified in various ways. A spiral spring for the plunger was substituted for the bow spring. The vertical action of the plunger was imparted through a reciprocating arm attached to a crank, and the loading spring was eliminated (Fig. 65).

Raisins, the dried form of sweet grapes, were used in mincemeat pies and in puddings and cakes. They were obtained in bulk from the grocer, and came complete with seeds, which were a nuisance if not removed before cooking. But unlike the cherry stoner, a mechanical raisin seeder was late in appearing. A simple hand tool for the purpose is illustrated by Franklin (1976, p. 176). It is like a hand-stamp, but the lower end has a grid of slightly curved wires, which stretch across and beneath the partly hollowed base. In use the device was pressed and rocked on a layer of raisins, probably soaked in advance. The seeds were squeezed out of the pulp and forced through the spaces between the wires.

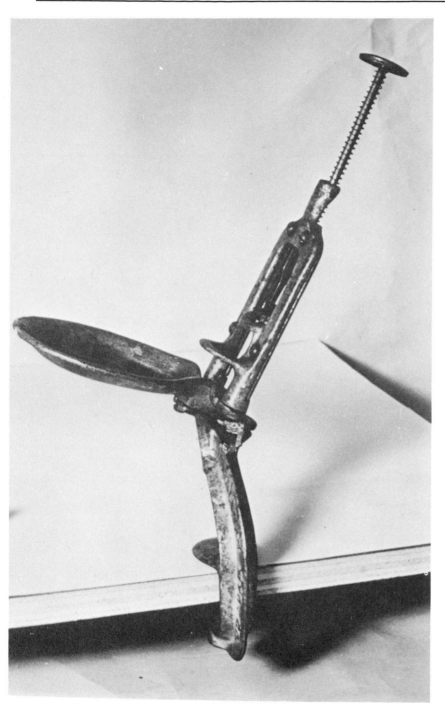

Fig. 64. Cherry stoner, Webster patent, 1870. National Museum of Man, Ottawa.

their three-pronged ends pierced the two cherries in the depressions and forced their stones through a perforated leather diaphragm in the hole, to fall into a dish below. The diverging points of the plungers retained the cherries on the up stroke, to be pulled off

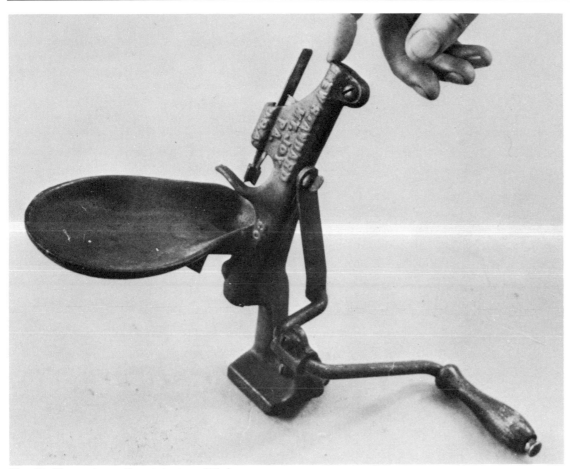

Fig. 65. Cherry stoner, Geer patent, modified.
National Museum of Man, Ottawa.

The principle appears in the mechanical seeder shown in Fig. 66. In this the wire grid is on the stationary part of the device. Raisins placed on it were squeezed by a metal plate, which swings forward and downward. The seeds were forced through the grid and the pulp was left behind to be scraped off. This seeder is based on the patent[48] issued in 1895 to Charles M. Fowler, of Springfield, Mass., but in his version the wire grid is on the hinged plate rather than on the stationary base. Also in 1895 a similar seeder was patented[49] by James H. Bullard of Springfield, but in this the wire grid is on the base and the presser is a small plate on a pivoted lever.

A different method of removing raisin seeds is used in the device shown in Fig. 67. This superficially resembles some of the meat grinders described previously. The case consists of an upper hopper and a lower chamber in which is mounted a horizontal cylinder attached to an external hand crank. This cylinder is made up of alternating large and small washers on a shaft, the large washers having toothed edges. Pressing against the cylinder is a rubber roller. Within each of the grooves formed in the cylinder by the small washers there is a loose metal ring, with a pointed extension projecting outward. In using this seeder, the wetted raisins are dropped into the hopper, from which they pass between the cylinder and the roller. Here the pulp is pressed into the grooves, leaving the seeds to be scraped off by the upper edge of a spout. The pulp is freed from the grooves by the projections ("doffers") of the loose rings, which being unattached to the cylinder, remain in one position while the cylinder revolves. The cast-iron stem supporting the seeder bears the raised inscription: ENTERPRISE M.F.G. CO. PHILADELPHIA P.A.

Fig. 66. Raisin seeder, Fowler patent, 1895. National Museum of Man, Ottawa. Photograph courtesy National Museums of Canada, Ottawa.

Fig. 67. Raisin seeder, Chase-Brown patents, 1895 and 1897, National Museum of Man, Ottawa.

USA PAT.APR.2. AUG.20.95 & OCT.5.97, and the admonition: WET THE RAISINS No. 36. The first date refers to the patent[50] of Frank H. Chase, Chicago, Illinois, and the last to that[51] of John W. Brown, Philadelphia, Pennsylvania. Another patent[52] for a raisin seeder was issued in 1897 to Cary S. Cox of Fresno, California.

Graters

A simple grater for producing cheese or vegetable shreds was made by punching holes in a piece of tin, so that the perforations projected on one side as a multitude of hollow points. Against these the object to be grated was scraped. The mechanical graters that appeared around the middle of the 19th century were mostly rotary versions of the punched-tin grater. Some, like the example shown in Fig. 68, were home-made. In this one the mechanism of an apple parer has been

Fig. 68. Home-made rotary grater, National Museum of Man, Ottawa.

mounted on the end of a stout wooden box. Secured to the apple fork is a tin can, which has been punched with numerous holes from the inside out. Food to be grated was held against the rotating can, and the gratings were removed by opening the box at its hinged front wall.

More sophisticated graters appeared toward the end of the century. These resemble the rotary meat grinder, but with a punched cylinder substituted for the spiral cutter (Fig. 69). The material to be grated was pressed into the hopper by means of a block of wood, and the gratings emerged at the end opposite the handle.

Graters were also used for spices, especially nutmeg, which was a popular spice in the 19th century. These woody, nut-like objects had to be grated for use in food or drink. The rotary graters described above could have been used for this purpose, but as only small amounts of nutmeg were used at any one time, it was usual to employ a miniature version of the punched-tin grater.

The most familiar nutmeg grater, which is still to be found in shops and kitchens, consists of a tapering half-cylinder, the convex side of which is the grater. The nutmeg kernel is rubbed back and forth on this, and the gratings fall into the interior and out the end. By the time that the nutmeg is worn down to a small size, there is a possibility of grating some finger also, and graters with some device to hold the kernel were devised. The first of these appeared in a patent[53] of 1854 issued to William Bradley of Lynn, Massachusetts. In this the hollow grater has a flat rasping surface, on which a cylindrical container can be slid back and forth. The kernel is held against the grating surface by a spring-loaded disc. The same principle applied to a semi-cylindrical grater appeared in the 1891 patent[54] of George H. Thomas, of Chicopee Falls, Massachusetts.

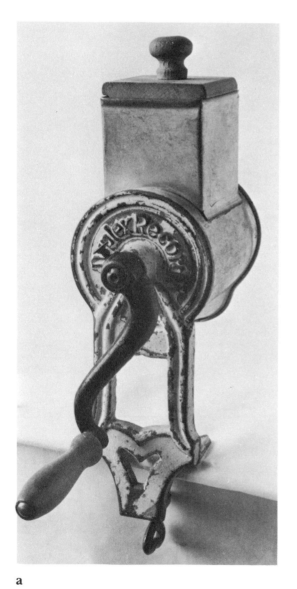

a

b

Fig. 69. Cheese grater, "Duplex Record": (a) operating position; (b) interior view showing grater. LSR Collection.

In his device the spring-loaded nutmeg holder is fixed at midlength of a metal strip, which is bent down at the ends to receive a narrow rod. On this rod the semicylindrical grating plate can be moved back and forth by means of a handle underneath. Also the nutmeg holder can be moved from side to side on the curved grating surface. A modified version of the same grater was patented[55] in 1896 by Charles E. Damon of Reading, Massachusetts. In this the nutmeg holder and the grating plate are held together by a simple wire frame. In the example shown (Fig. 70) the nutmeg holder is stamped: THE EDGAR,

with the two patent dates, Damon assigned his patent to the Edgar Manufacturing Company of Reading.

Presses

Lemon juice was and is a popular flavoring for food and drink, but squeezing lemons by hand is a messy job. Simple presses for this purpose, called lemon squeezers, were in use before the mid-century. They were made of two pieces of wood hinged on each other and

Fig. 70. Nutmeg grater, Thomas-Damon patents, 1891 and 1896. LSR Collection.

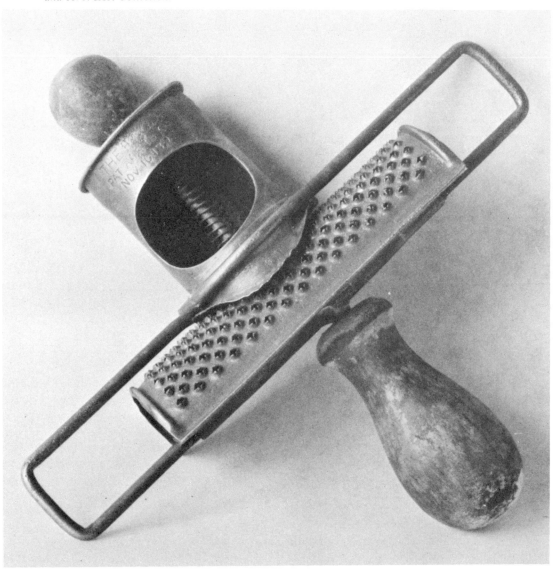

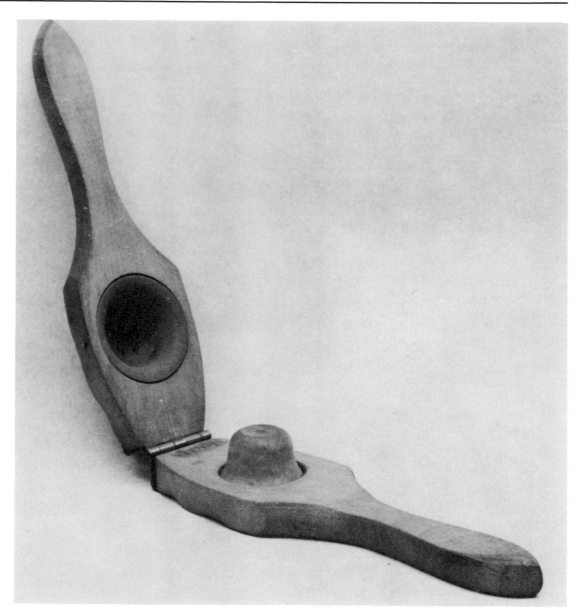

Fig. 71. Wooden lemon squeezer, Black Creek Pioneer
Village, Toronto.

shaped as handles at the unhinged end (Fig. 71). One piece has a bowl-shaped hollow to receive the half-lemon, the other a dome-shaped plunger. When the two parts were squeezed together by means of the handles, the lemon juice ran out through perforations and was caught in a receptacle. Squeezers of cast iron using the same principle appeared in 1860. In the patent[56] of L. S. Chichester, New York, N.Y., the bowl and plunger are cone-shaped. Curved shapes reappeared in the metal squeezer patented[57] in 1862 by G. M. Thomas of Troy, N.Y. In the 1867 patent[58] of Thomas Reece and Arthur Clarke, Philadelphia, Pa., the two jaws hinged on a fulcrum, like pliers.

Simple lemon squeezers of this kind were still being made and sold in the 1890s. Some were entirely of cast iron (Fig. 72), others had an iron bowl and a wooden plunger, and still others had the squeezing parts made of porcelain. Perforations in the plunger permitted the juice to flow out while retaining the seeds and pulp. The familiar glass lemon squeezer, with ribbed dome and juice-catching rim, was advertised in the Sears, Roebuck catalogue of 1897.

Some type of press was used to force sausage meat into the "case". A simple device for this purpose (Fig. 73) consists of a sheet-metal cylinder, tapering at one end as a funnel into a narrow spout. A wooden plunger, with handle, fits into the cylinder. The sausage case, a length of washed pig intestine, was tied over the spout, and sausage meat in the cylinder was forced into the case by pushing on the plunger. Something larger than this sausage "gun" was needed when sausage-making was done on a community scale. A common version (Fig. 74) consists of a wooden box, square in cross-section, and open at the top. This box is mounted at about the midlength of a narrow, four-legged bench. An upright at one end of the bench supports a long lever, from which a wooden piston hangs down to fit into the open box. Sausage meat, placed in the box, was pressed by the lever and piston, and forced out through a spout into the sausage case. To withstand the pressure, the box was usually reinforced with iron straps.

From this it was a logical step to a

Fig. 72. Iron lemon squeezer, Black Creek Pioneer Village, Toronto.

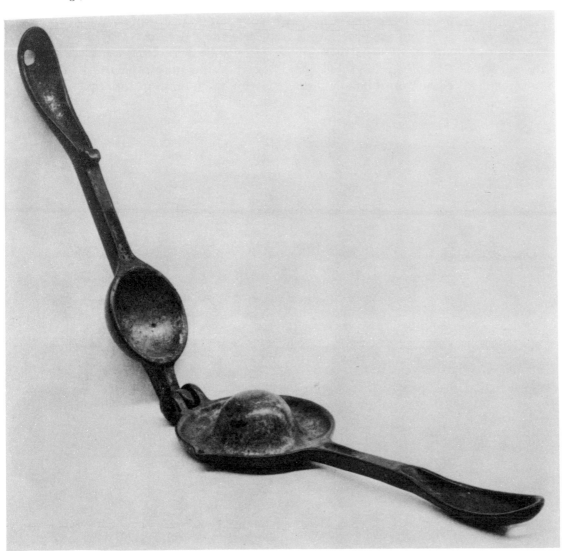

sausage stuffer with a metal container, and this appeared in the patent[59] of 1848 issued to Seneca S. Jones of Leicester, N.Y. In this the meat container is an iron cylinder attached to a wooden base and opening below into a spout at an angle of 45°. Over this spout is slipped a close-fitting tube, with grooves on the inner side. As with the wooden stuffer, the meat is forced out of the container and into the case by means of a piston ("follower") suspended from a lever. The object of the grooves in the outlet tube is to allow air to escape from the sausage case during filling. A sausage stuffer of this type is on display in the Henry Ford Museum at Dearborn, Michigan, together with a similar stuffer in which the outlet is directly downward through the wooden bench on which the cylinder sits.

Different in appearance but operating on the same principle is the sausage stuffer patented[60] in 1858 by J. G. Perry of South Kingston, Rhode Island (Fig. 75). In this the meat container is a heavy cast-iron tube, bent in a 90° curve, and mounted with the open end up, the other end, tapering to a spout, directed horizontally. A long iron lever, with a hinged piston, is attached at the top, and with this the sausage meat was forced through the spout. The Perry sausage stuffer is shown in the 1897 Sears, Roebuck catalogue.

Late in the 19th century, sausage presses came on the market in which the piston was operated by a vertical screw or a rack and pinion. The best known of these are the various models made by the Enterprise Manufacturing Company (Fig. 76). Small presses had a simple screw-type piston, operated by a handle at the top. The medium-sized press worked with a rack and pinion, connected to a crank at the side. The large size had a screw-type piston, turned by means of gears and a crank. In all models the outlet was at the base of the cylindrical container. The smaller models were intended also for use in squeezing juice from fruit, and for preparing tinctures in pharmacies.

a

b

Fig. 73. Hand-operated sausage stuffer: (a) closed position; (b) with piston removed. LSR Collection.

*Fig. 74. Wooden sausage stuffer, Black Creek Pioneer
Village, Toronto.*

Sugar Utensils

Domestic sweetening early in the 19th century
was provided mostly by molasses and brown
sugar, both imported from the West Indies
in large barrels. Devices used to dispense these
substances were designed primarily for the
retail trade, but might have been required by
large households. Molasses was drawn off
from the barrel through some sort of tap.
Being a viscid liquid it was likely to drip from
an ordinary spigot. By the late 1830s a device
called a molasses gate became available. In

*Fig. 75. Sausage stuffer, Perry patent, 1858. National
Museum of Man, Ottawa.*

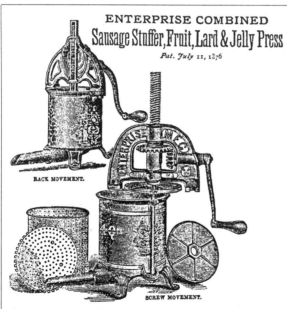

ENTERPRISE COMBINED
Sausage Stuffer, Fruit, Lard & Jelly Press

Pat. July 11, 1876

RACK MOVEMENT.

SCREW MOVEMENT.

The above cuts represent our Sausage Stuffers, Fruit, Lard and Jelly Presses combined.
They are decidedly the easiest working and most durable machines ever manufactured, and
will be found very useful for many purposes in every family.

DIRECTIONS.—When in operation, the pressure applied will remain without holding
the crank. When the plunger is raised so as to clear the top of the cylinder, it can be readily swung around, so that the press can be filled or emptied. For pressing fruit or lard,
the cylinder and bottom (as shown in cut) are to be placed in the press.

☞ *A Cloth or Bag should be used when pressing fruit or jelly, to prevent
the pulp or seeds from passing through the holes in the strainer.*

For stuffing sausages, the tin strainer and bottom plate are to be removed. There are two
plunger plates with each machine—the larger one for stuffing, and the smaller one for pressing. They can be easily exchanged by screwing them on or off.

PRICES.

No. 5—2 Qt. Japanned; Rack, $2.00   No. 25—4 Qt. Japanned, Screw, $5.00
   10—2 " Galvanized "   3.50   30—4 " Galvanized "   7.00
   15—2 " Japanned, Screw, 3.50   35—8 " Japanned, "   7.50
   20—2 " Galvanized, "   5.00   40—8 " Galvanized "   10.50

PACKED AS DESIRED.

ENTERPRISE
TINCTURE PRESS.

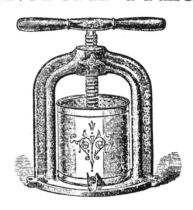

The above illustration represents our Tincture and Wine Press,
which we guarantee superior to any in the market.

Druggists will find it very suitable for their wants.

PRICES.

1 Quart,	$3.75
2 "	5.00
4 "	7.50
8 "	10.00

PACKED AS DESIRED.

*Fig. 76. Mechanical presses, Enterprise Mfg. Co.
catalogue, 1878. Pennsylvania Historical
Society, Philadelphia.*

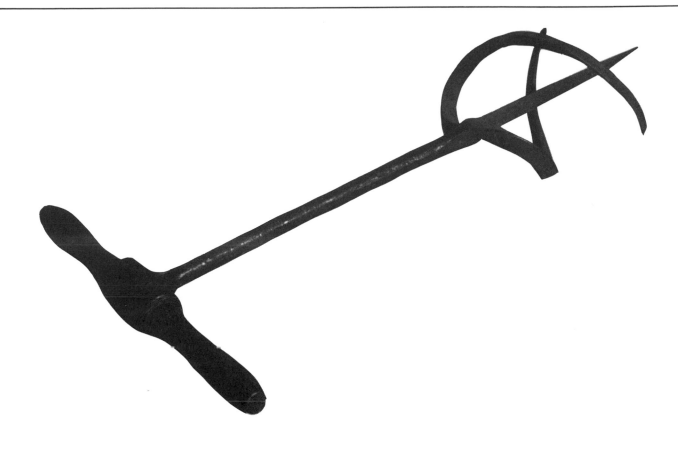

*Fig. 77. Sugar auger, National Museum of Man,
Ottawa.*

this a small plate attached to a handle could be brought down across the tap opening to cut off the flow completely. A molasses gate was advertised in the Enterprise Manufacturing Co. catalogue for 1878 but in their 1883 catalogue it was replaced by a measuring faucet, in which a calibrated dial registered the amount of molasses delivered by turning a crank.

Brown sugar came in solid form but soft and moist. As it remained in storage it dried and hardened, making it difficult to remove. The tool commonly used to deal with this situation was the sugar auger (Fig. 77), which looks like a giant corkscrew. It has a spike-like shaft with a transverse wooden handle, much like a carpenter's auger, but in addition there are two spiral spikes taking off from the shaft. In use the point of the shaft was driven into the sugar mass and the tool twisted. The spiral spikes bit into the sugar, freeing a portion which was pulled out by lifting the auger.

Sugar came in other forms. Demerara sugar was a brown variety but crystalline, so that it did not dry and solidify. White sugar was sold in tall conical form, the sugar loaf. The reason for this shape was that in the evaporation of the purified sugar syrup there was a liquid residue called treacle. To remove this the wet sugar crystals were placed in narrow, conical funnels and allowed to drain. The result was a dry but very hard cone of sugar. To break off a portion for use, sugar shears were commonly used (Fig. 78). These were like tongs, but with the ends of the jaws expanded into cutting blades. With this device the housewife could snip off pieces

Fig. 78. Sugar shears, Black Creek Pioneer Village, Toronto.

of sugar from the loaf. By the 1860s, devices for cutting the sugar loaf into pieces of practical size were patented for use by retail merchants, and the sugar was sold in that form to the consumer. White sugar was usually reserved for serving with tea. The use of vacuum processes for refining white sugar eventually made granulated sugar available, and the sugar loaf disappeared from the trade.

Ice-cream Freezers

The making of frozen confections goes back to ancient times but these were the luxury of the wealthy. Presumably they were made by stirring some suitable mixture in a vessel surrounded by ice and salt. In the 19th century, mechanical ice-cream freezers were developed, and this delicious dessert could be made wherever ice was available. According to Franklin (1976, p. 125) "The first freezer is supposed to have been invented by Nancy Johnson in 1846. Her freezer was granted a patent in 1848, but to a William Young".[61] W. G. Young of Baltimore, Md., did obtain the first U.S. patent for an ice-

cream freezer in 1848, and in his specifications states: "The best now in use is that known as 'Johnston's' [sic], which is like the ordinary freezer, with a revolving shaft inside it, on which are two curved wings that move around and cause the cream to revolve in the freezer and be thrown to the outside". This describes a prototype of the common ice-cream freezer, described below. Young's patent, however, was very different. Agitation inside the freezer was obtained by means of a vertical plunger. There were two large handles attached to the cream container, which allowed it to be turned in the ice tub while the plunger was being operated.

The basic ice-cream freezer (Fig. 79) consists of two cylindrical vessels, the inner of sheet metal, the outer of wood or metal. The space between is wide enough for the introduction of a mixture of crushed ice and salt. The inner cylinder has a tight-fitting lid through which a rotating shaft projects. Inside the cylinder this shaft bears a series of horizontal paddles. Outside, the shaft is connected to a crank, either directly or through a set of gears. In 1848 H. B. Masser of Sunbury, Pa., patented[62] an ice-cream freezer in which the cream container and its enclosed paddles were made to revolve in opposite directions by means of a bevel pinion and two bevel gears, one above and one below the pinion. Masser's freezer had the additional innovation of a hollow shaft for the paddles, into which crushed ice and salt could be introduced. Many variations of the "Johnston" freezer appeared during the 19th century. A typical example is that advertised by Sidney Shepard & Co. of Buffalo in their catalogue of 1888 on pages 38 and 39 (Fig. 80). It is said to have been patented July 9, 1872 and July 13, 1875. These patents[63] were issued to J. W. Condon of Logansport, Indiana. The cream container was made to revolve through bevel gears from a crank. The paddle ("dasher") was fixed, and had an adjustable wooden blade to scrape the ice-cream from the wall of the cylinder, to which it might freeze. Shepard ice-cream freezers were illustrated in the Sears, Roebuck catalogue of 1897.

A nostalgic description of the ice-cream freezer in use is given by Gould,[64] and the account fits my own childhood memories, including the fun of scraping the remnants of the frozen custard from the paddle blades.

Churns

Butter is made by coalescing the fat globules in cream. To separate the cream from the whole milk, the latter was placed in shallow bowls or pans, in a cool place. When the milk was cooled the cream rose to the surface. It was skimmed off by means of a shallow wooden paddle, a large spoon, or latterly by a tin skimmer (Fig. 81), which is a slightly concave scoop with perforations to let the milk run through while retaining the thicker cream. In hot weather, when chilling the milk might be difficult, the cream could be made to rise by heating the whole milk.

The use of centrifugal force to separate the cream from milk was introduced in the De Laval cream separator, a Swedish invention. It appeared in North America at the International Dairy Fair in New York, 1879. The early models were large, and intended for use in butter factories. By the

a

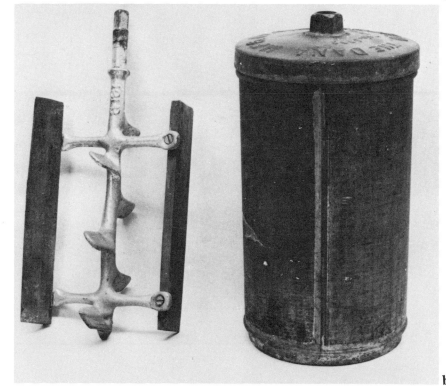

b

Fig. 79. Ice-cream freezer: (a) external view; (b) cream container and dasher. Black Creek Pioneer Village, Toronto.

38   SIDNEY SHEPARD & CO.

CHAMPION ICE CREAM FREEZERS.

Patented July 9, 1872; July 13, 1875.

GEARED.   FLY WHEEL.

Heavy Tin Cylinders.

		Each.
No. 19.	2 qts.	$3.75
No. 20.	3 qts.	4.50
No. 21.	4 qts.	5.50
No. 22.	6 qts.	7.00
No. 23.	8 qts.	9.00
No. 24.	10 qts.	11.00
No. 25.	12 qts.	14.00
No. 26.	16 qts.	17.00
No. 27.	20 qts.	23.00

Heavy Tin Cylinders.

		Each.
No. 28.	16 qts.	$21.00
No. 29.	20 qts.	28.00
No. 30.	32 qts.	40.00
No. 31.	40 qts.	45.00

SEPARATE PARTS.

TOP PLATE.   DASHER.   CYLINDER.
Galvanized Iron.   Galvanized Iron.   Heavy Tin.
                    Adjustable Wood Scraper.   Galvanized Iron Cover and Bottom.

We introduced these Freezers in 1873, and they have given general satisfaction. They have been placed in the hands of families, confectioners and hotels and thoroughly tested and approved by them. We have made such improvements in the mechanical construction as our own experience and that of practical ice cream makers has suggested, making them in every respect

THE BEST FREEZERS YET PRODUCED

Fig. 80. Ice-cream freezers, catalogue of Sidney
Shepard & Co., Buffalo, New York, 1888.
Courtesy of The Henry Ford Museum,
Dearborn, Michigan.

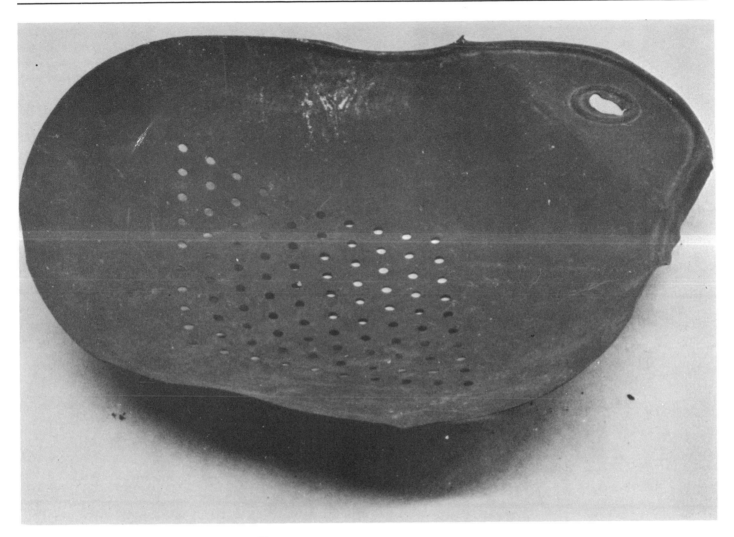

Fig. 81. Cream skimmer, Black Creek Pioneer Village, Toronto.

1890s, small versions operated by a hand crank were available for home use. The whine of the whirling mechanism, and the change in pitch as the separation began, were familiar sounds in the farm kitchen.

Very good butter can be made from sweet cream, but the process is easier if the cream is sour. This sourness is produced by the bacterial fermentation of the milk sugar to produce lactic acid. Milk or cream that has not been treated to kill the normal bacteria will become sour in a warm place over night. To make butter the separated cream is agitated vigorously. This causes the tiny fat globules to collide and adhere to each other, eventually coalescing into a more or less solid mass. Almost any method of agita-

tion will work, but the most common was by means of a vertical plunger in a dasher churn (Fig. 82). This is a tall, narrow container of wood or crockery, with a perforated lid. Through this perforation a wooden rod, like a broom handle, extends from interior to exterior. At the lower end of the rod, inside the churn, a wooden cross is attached, formed of two slats joined together like the shape of the Red Cross emblem. With the churn partly filled with sour cream, the rod (dasher) was moved up and down vigorously. Increased resistance to the dasher indicated that lumps of butter were forming. These were removed by hand, washed and pressed into a solid mass, while the thin residual liquid called buttermilk was discarded, or fed to the pigs,

Fig. 82. Dasher churn, National Museum of Man,
Ottawa.

or cooled and drunk as a beverage.

Operating a dasher churn was tiring, and the amount of butter produced was small in proportion to the effort. The operation was made less tedious, but probably no quicker, by using a complicated wooden device (Fig. 83) on which the operator sat, and pulled a pair of horizontal handles as if rowing a boat. By a series of levers this motion was transmitted to the dasher, causing it to move up and down.

Tread-mills ("dog powers") were used as the source of motive power for churns. There were two types, a sloping belt of slats and canvas, on which the animal walked (Fig. 84), or a hollow drum of wooden slats within which the dog ran like a squirrel in its rotary cage (Fig. 85). Large dogs, such as border collies, were used with these tread mills, and one farmer recalled that his old dog

recognized the early signs of churning and tried vainly to disappear. A dog power similar to that shown in Fig. 84 was patented in 1867[65] by Matthew Cummings of Bridgewater, Canada West (Ontario). Intended primarily to operate a washing machine, it was provided with a coupling for a dasher churn. Dog powers are illustrated in the Sears, Roebuck catalogue of 1897, and came in two sizes, for a single dog or for two. The descriptive text is interesting. "This power can be operated by a dog, goat or sheep; yields 25 per cent more power from a given weight of animal than any other, and with adjustable bridge to regulate the required power and motion, a 30 pound animal will do the churning; if you keep a dog, make him 'work his passage'." The rotary motion produced by these tread mills was most suited to rotary churns, but could be adapted to a dasher

Fig. 83. Churning machine, Black Creek Pioneer Village, Toronto.

Fig. 84. Dog-power, Doon Pioneer Village, Kitchener, Ontario.

Fig. 85. Dog-power, Black Creek Pioneer Village, Toronto.

churn by means of a walking beam.

Rotary motion was used in a wide variety of churns. The simplest was a rectangular or cylindrical container of wood or tin, in which a reel-like device with four paddles was turned by means of an external handle (Fig. 86). Box churns without internal paddles were used. The box was mounted on a frame and could be rotated rapidly by means of a handle. In some examples, the axis of rotation was from one corner of the box to the opposite corner (Fig. 87). Churns in which the container was a barrel were common in the late 19th century. Some were mounted with a handle, for simple rotation, while others could be given a rocking motion by means of a lever.

My own experiments seem to indicate that the quickest method of producing butter is by means of a back-and-forth shaking motion. This was provided in the rocker churn, a rectangular container with curved bottom and ends (Fig. 88). It is pivoted at midlength on a frame, and by means of a handle at one end, like that of a baby carriage, it can be rocked vigorously from end to end. The flat top has an opening with a lid, and through this the cream was introduced and the butter removed. The buttermilk was drawn off through a hole with plug at the bottom of the churn.

A similar sloshing motion was produced in the swinging churn (Fig. 88), which was suspended from the ceiling. A distinctive version of such a churn was patented[66] in 1874 by John Campbell of Almonte, Ontario. This is a sheet-metal cylinder about two feet long and 18 inches in diameter, with the ends extended as conical funnels. There is a rectangular opening in the top, with tight-fitting lid, a hand-grip at one end and a plugged opening at the other, and four short legs to support the churn when not in use. Internally there are partial partitions to help break up the cream and a small paddle wheel to supplement the agitation. On the top of the churn are two iron loops, one at each end of the opening. Rods were attached to these, with the other end suspended from rafter or ceiling. Charged with sour cream, the churn was swung back and forth on its long axis. After the butter had formed the churn was lowered to the floor, the plug removed and the buttermilk drained off by tilting, and the

Fig. 86. Box churn, National Museum of Man, Ottawa.

butter scooped out through the rectangular opening in the top.

Hundreds of patents were issued in the United States and Canada during the 19th century for "improvements" and attachments for churns. Many of these were intended for use in large dairies or butter factories. A miniature churn did appear in the 1890s that was suitable for domestic use. It consisted of an eggbeater mechanism set into the lid of a large, rectangular jar.

The term "atmospheric churn" appears in a number of patents in 1848. The earliest of these[67] was issued to Nathan Chapin of Cortlandville, N.Y., but he did not claim priority for the use of air bubbles to supplement the agitation of the paddles. The innovation was in the use of trough-shaped paddles, which on rotation would carry air

from the surface to the bottom of the cream and there release it to ascend as bubbles. Other atmospheric churns of the late 1840s and the 1850s introduced the air stream through a hollow dasher or blades, or through an opening for the output of a small air pump operated by the churn drive. Interest in the atmospheric churn seems to have died down in the 1860s.

Freshly churned butter contains disseminated buttermilk, which must be removed to obtain a good flavor and prevent spoilage. With small amounts of butter this was done by washing it in cold water, then squeezing and pressing it in a wooden bowl with a curved paddle (Fig. 89). With large amounts of butter this would be too tedious, and more elaborate butter-working devices were used. A common type that has survived

Fig. 87. Box and rotary churns, Chateau de Ramezay, Montreal.

Fig. 88. Rocking churn and swinging churns,
Campbell patent, 1874. National Museum
of Man, Ottawa.

in numerous examples is a kind of three-legged table, the triangular top of which slopes toward one of the legs (Fig. 90). The two sloping edges have low walls, which do not meet at the lower end, leaving an opening through which the squeezed-out buttermilk could drain. The pressing was done with a kind of rolling pin, the lower end of which is pivoted at the low corner of the table, and the upper end provided with a handle. Butter placed on the flat top was squeezed by rolling the pin from side to side in an arc-like path. As with churns, there were many patented butter workers, mostly more suited to the factory than to the home. A common type had

a rectangular table and a cylindrical roller, mounted so as to be rolled from end to end over the butter, while the pressed-out buttermilk drained through an opening on one side of the table.

For domestic use, butter was commonly stored in crockery jars, but for sale it was pressed into convenient brick-shaped blocks weighing approximately one pound. These were made in simple presses, consisting of a rectangular wooden box, open at the bottom, with a loose top that could be pushed down by means of a handle. Butter was spooned into the open bottom, the press placed on a table, and the butter squeezed by pushing down on the lid. The operation was repeated until the mould would hold no more, then the brick of butter was pushed out and wrapped for handling.

For use in the home, butter was pressed in small cylindrical moulds, with the face of the piston having some incised design, such as a heart, a flower, or the American eagle. This was imparted in relief to the surface of the pressed butter. For table servings small portions of butter were formed into spherical "patties" by rolling them with a circular motion between two corrugated wooden paddles.

Fig. 89. Burl bowl and butter paddle, National Museum of Man, Ottawa.

Fig. 90. Butter worker, Black Creek Pioneer Village, Toronto.

Lighting

The story of domestic lighting in North America during the 19th century has been told elsewhere. The concern here is not so much with the techniques of illumination as in the way in which the preparation and care of lighting devices were made easier and more effective.

North American interiors, at the beginning of the 19th century, were illuminated mainly by the candle or the whale-oil lamp. The newly invented Argand lamp, with its circular flame and glass chimney, was still too expensive to have much general use. Most home lighting was not much different from that of medieval Europe.

Candles

Domestic candles of the 18th century were made of tallow, the concentrated fat of sheep or cattle, with or without some additive to make them more rigid. Tallow candles were made in the home by two methods, moulding and dipping. Making candles in moulds was a straightforward operation. The tubular moulds were strung with the wick cord, and then filled with melted tallow, which was allowed to cool and harden. The candles could then be pulled out after dipping the mould in hot water. Usually the tubes were arranged in parallel rows (Fig. 91), but in some examples they were mounted in a circle, which may have made pouring a little easier. But there was not much room for invention here.

Candle-making by dipping was done by repeatedly immersing wicks in melted tallow, with intervals of cooling and solidification between. Usually a number of wicks were suspended from a stick and dipped together, then hung between chair-backs while the tallow congealed (Fig. 92). Some sort of rotary rack for the dipped wicks helped to

speed the operation. The usual device was a square block of wood mounted so as to rotate on the top of a vertical shaft. There is a hole on each side of the block, into which the ends of the wick sticks can be inserted. In use, each stick was removed from the block in turn, the wicks dipped, and the stick inserted again with the wicks dangling. The block was then turned to the next stick and the operation repeated. By the time the block was revolved once, the tallow on the first set of wicks had congealed, and was ready for another dip. In some versions of the rotary rack the wicks were suspended from circular blocks of wood, which were in turn attached to the rotary arms by a hook and eye.

A more elaborate candle-dipping machine (Fig. 93) was made in 1846 by a Canadian pioneer, John Langton, for his sister Anne in their home on Sturgeon Lake,

Fig. 91. Candle holder, candle mould, and extinguisher. National Museum of Man, Ottawa.

Fig. 92. Dipped candles, Officers' Quarters, Fort York, Toronto.

Upper Canada. Langton went on to become the first Auditor General of Canada. As sketched by Anne, the device looks like a miniature Ferris wheel. It had a circular frame revolving in a vertical plane. Twelve pairs of radial arms had short bars pivoted from their ends. Each pair of bars was joined at the free ends by a transverse rod, from which the candle wicks were suspended. The melted tallow, in a narrow, deep container, was set up across one side of the device, parallel to the wick rods. The operator lifted up one rod with its wicks, dipped the wicks in the tallow, and then allowed them to fall back into the suspended position. The frame was then rotated, the next row of wicks dipped, and so on. In spite of its ingenuity and

effectiveness, the Langton dipping machine seems to have been unique.

Most candle holders were metal sockets mounted on a base (Fig. 91). Often there was a device for adjusting the height of the candle. This consisted of an internal piston connected through a vertical slot to an external handle. With this arrangement only a small amount of candle needed to project from the socket, preventing collapse of the tallow in a warm room. Another device for the same purpose was a spirally slotted socket, made by twisting a strip of iron into a loose coil. A small metal disc with handle, engaged in the slot, could be used to raise the candle by moving it in the slot, on the principle of the Archimedes screw.

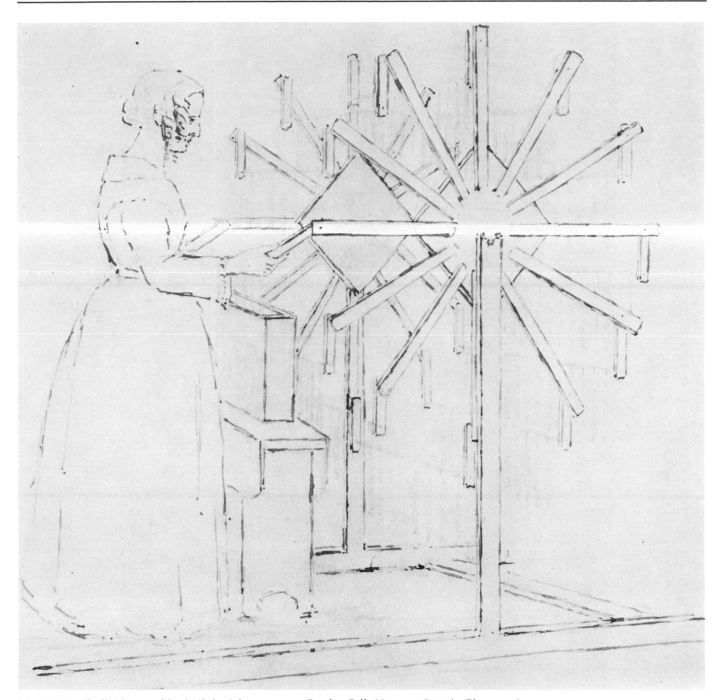

Fig. 93. Candle-dipping machine built by John Langton, Sturgeon Lake, Canada West, 1846. From a drawing by Anne Langton in the Fenelon Falls Museum, Ontario. Photograph by Leigh Warren, Royal Ontario Museum.

Oil Lamps

The Argand lamp,[1] invented by Ami Argand about 1782 in Montpelier, France, was an enormous advance over the simple oil lamp with a cord-like wick projecting through a short tube. In the Argand burner the wick is hose-shaped, and is supported between a smaller and a larger metal tube. The inner tube is separated from the fuel chamber and is open below, so that air can enter and rise to ventilate the inner side of the circular flame. At first the Argand wick was adjusted with a pointed iron stylus, the wick pick, as with the simple oil lamp. A major improvement came in 1819 with the invention[2] of Nicolas Conne of London of the spiral wick raiser. This was an adaptation from the spirally slotted candle holder. In the Conne device the inner draft tube was spirally grooved, and attached to an external knob so that it could be turned. A short, tubular wick holder fitted over the grooved tube, with an internal stud to engage the groove. An external stud filled into a vertical groove in the outer tube of the burner. When the inner tube was turned, the wick holder could only move up and down, because of the vertical groove in which it was engaged. Wick raisers of this sort were used with Argand-type lamps to the end of the 19th century (Fig. 94).

Lard Lamps

As the better grades of whale oil became prohibitively expensive in the 1840s, new lamp fuels came into use. Among these were lard and lard oil. Lard is the solidified fat

Fig. 94. Argand lamp, ca. 1830 (drawing): (a) complete lamp; (b) shade removed to show burner. Original found in New Brunswick Museum, Saint John.

a

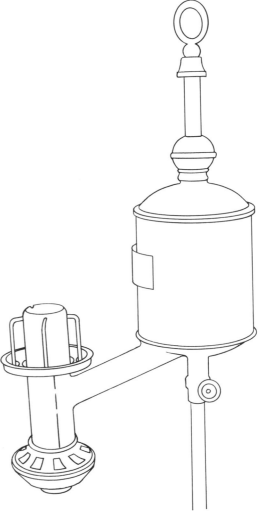

b

*Fig. 95. Lard lamp, Southworth patent, 1842. U.S.
National Museum of History and
Technology, Washington, D.C.*

of pigs and requires melting to serve as a lamp fuel. Even lard oil, the more fluid constituent of lard, is viscous at ordinary temperatures. The many ingenious lard lamps that appeared between 1840 and 1860 were designed to overcome this difficulty of poor flow. One of the earliest and simplest was the Southworth lamp[3] of 1842, in which there are two flat wicks with an air draft between, a modification of the Argand principle (Fig. 95). The wick tubes are of copper, and there is an additional copper strip between, all designed to conduct heat from burner to fuel. To start a lamp of this sort one primed the wicks with some lard in the priming cup around the burner. Once started, the flame

Fig. 96. Lard lamp, based on Davis patent, 1856.
LSR Collection.

quickly produced enough heat to melt some of the lard in the font. A true Argand lard lamp (Fig. 96), with tubular wick, was patented[4] in 1856 by Samuel Davis of New Holland, Pa. The most popular lard lamp seems to have been that invented in 1851 by Delamar Kinnear of Circleville, Ohio.[5] This has a very broad, flat wick tube, a wide, thin font shaped like an axe head, and a small tube for a pilot wick (Fig. 97). Early Kinnear

Fig. 97. Lard lamp, Kinnear patent, 1851. LSR Collection.

lamps have a sliding top for filling the font, but later models have a circular opening with a cap.

An alternate method of making lard flow is to apply pressure. This was done in the Maltby and Neal lamp[6] of 1842. In this (Fig. 98) the two wick tubes are enclosed in a cylindrical plunger, which can be pushed down into the fuel font, thus forcing the lard up into the vicinity of the burner. In 1854, I. Smith and J. Stonesifer of Boonsborough, Maryland, patented[7] a lard lamp with a separate fuel reservoir, having a screw-actuated piston to force the lard out through an opening at the base into the adjacent font with the burner (Fig. 99). D.H. Chamberlain, of Boston, Mass., obtained a patent[8] in 1854 for a lard lamp with a cylindrical font, which can be rotated, thus

using gravity to keep the partly melted lard in contact with the wicks (Fig. 100).

The elegant solar lamps (Fig. 101) that appeared in the 1840s, mostly from Philadelphia manufacturers, were a form of Argand lamp designed to burn whale oil. The burner, with its tubular wick and Conne wick raiser, is mounted directly on the brass font, which is shaped like a depressed sphere. There is a low, broad draft deflector around the burner, which is said to have produced a high, narrow flame, aided by the draft of the tall, almost tubular chimney. In addition, the solar lamp usually came with a globular, ornamented glass shade.

The discovery that solar lamps worked well with lard oil and even with lard, led to a brief popularity just before the introduction of kerosene. Robert Cornelius, one of the Philadelphia lamp makers, patented[9] a special deflector in 1843, designed to conduct heat down to the fuel. Even without this the all-metal construction of the solar lamp seems to have provided sufficient melting to make the lard flow. But solar lamps

Fig. 98. Lard lamp, Maltby and Neal patent, 1842: (a) extended position; (b) compressed position. Private collection.

a

b

Fig. 99. Lard lamp, Smith and Stonesifer, 1854. U.S. National Museum of History and Technology, Washington, D.C.

using lard required frequent cleaning of the burner.

Burning-fluid Lamps

The alternate substitute for whale oil as a lamp fuel was burning fluid, often erroneously called camphene. As originally patented[10] in 1830 by Isaiah Jennings of New York, N.Y., it consisted of 95% alcohol with a small proportion of purified turpentine (the real camphene). The same mixture was patented[11] one year later in Canada by John Ratcliff of Odelltown, probably by arrangement with Jennings. The new fuel was inexpensive, clean, very fluid, and it burned with a smokeless white flame. However, due to its high volatility, it was dangerous to use, causing many fires and

Fig. 100. Lard lamp, Chamberlain patent, 1854.
           Hastings County Museum, Belleville,
           Ontario.

a

b

c

*Fig. 101. Solar lamp, ca. 1845: (a) entire lamp
(chimney not original), Royal Ontario
Museum photograph; (b) with shade and
chimney removed; (c) with deflector
removed. LSR Collection.*

explosions. Nevertheless, it was manufactured in many millions of gallons in the 1840s and 1850s. Lamps for burning fluid resemble whale-oil lamps but are higher and narrower, to reduce vaporization (Fig. 102). The glass is thick, and being press-moulded, incorporated attractive designs. The burners are distinctive. In place of the short, wide wick tubes of the whale-oil lamp, which project down into the font, these burners have narrow, tapering and diverging tubes, with no extension below. Each tube is provided with a cap, to prevent evaporation and serve as an extinguisher.

Many ingenious but mostly ineffective devices were patented in the burning-fluid period in attempts to reduce the dangers of this fuel. Few have survived as compared with the numerous conventional burning-fluid lamps, so they evidently were not very popular. One that apparently had some sale was the invention of John Newell of Boston, patented[12] in 1853. In this the wicks within the font are enclosed in a cylinder of silver-plated brass gauze. This could have had little effect in reducing the danger of excessive vaporization. Probably more effective was the 1855 patented[13] lamp of William Bennett, of Brooklyn, N.Y.; in this the fluid was contained in a rubber bag within the glass font, permitting expansion without rupture. Bennett lamps were offered for sale in 1856.

Kerosene Lamps

A new lamp fuel was made and demonstrated in 1846 by Dr. Abraham Gesner, of Chipman Corner, Nova Scotia. Subsequently he named it kerosene. Two years later the Scottish chemist James Young produced the same substance and called it paraffine oil. It was made by distilling bituminous coal or oil shale at a temperature below that used in making illuminating gas. For this reason it was often called coal oil. Kerosene from coal was on the market by 1855. It was almost

Fig. 102. Burning-fluid lamp, ca. 1850, with original wick. LSR Collection.

as expensive as whale oil, and so did not become popular until 1860, with the development of petroleum production in Western Pennsylvania and southwestern Ontario. Petroleum was a cheaper and better source of kerosene than coal, and the price dropped to about one-quarter of its previous level. For the next 20 years the kerosene lamp was the almost universal source of domestic light.

Kerosene lamps of the late 1850s and early 1860s resemble a combination of the solar lamp and the burning-fluid lamp (Fig. 103). Like the latter they have a glass font, but in shape this is more like the metal font of the solar lamp, and the brass stem and marble base were derived directly from one style of solar lamp. Many solar lamps were converted to kerosene by closing the space at the top of the font with a brass washer having a threaded collar to receive the kerosene burner.

A burner especially suited to the kerosene lamp appeared in North America about 1856. It was manufactured in Austria and was sold under the name of Vienna burner. The wick is ribbon-shaped, and is raised and lowered in the flat wick tube by means of a toothed wheel, which is turned by an external thumb wheel. The most distinctive feature is the dome-shaped draft deflector with its narrow slot for the frame. This concentrated the rising draft on the burning wick. Outside its rim of the deflector is a collar-like socket for the base of the cylindrical glass chimney.

By 1858, burners of the Vienna type were being patented and made in the United States. Many of the "improvements" were trivial, but in 1861 Carleton Newman of Pittsburgh introduced a hinged burner,[14] in which the combined deflector and chimney holder could be swung upward and outward to expose the wick for trimming. The same device appears in the burner patented by Albert Taplin,[15] of Providence, R.I., in 1862, and by John J. Marcy[16] of Meriden, Conn., in 1863. These differ in details of the

Fig. 103. Kerosene lamp with Jones patent burner, 1858. LSR Collection.

a

b

Fig. 104. Kerosene burner, Marcy patent, 1863: (a) deflector and chimney holder in place; (b) deflector and chimney holder swung on hinge. LSR Collection.

Fig. 105. "Fireside" Kerosene burner, Atwood patent, 1873. LSR Collection.

hinge (Fig. 104). The familiar kerosene burner, still being made and sold, with the hinged deflector and the four long, springy prongs to hold the chimney, was patented[17] in 1873 by L.J. Atwood of Waterbury, Conn. (Fig. 105). A characteristic burner of the 1860s was that patented[18] by Michael H. Collins of Chelsea, Mass., in 1865. In this (Fig. 106) the deflector is a low dome, extended outward as a rim of springy, petal-like blades. The chimney, usually a plain glass cylinder, was pushed down around this retaining rim to rest on the basal edge of the burner.

Fig. 106. Kerosene burner, Collins patent, 1865. LSR
Collection.

During the 1860s the Argand burner went into temporary decline. Even the "student" lamp, patented[19] in 1863 by Carl A. Kleeman of Erfurt, Prussia, and a simple adaptation of the original Argand, was almost unknown until it was reintroduced in 1870 (Fig. 107). In the decade that followed, the Argand principle was exploited in a number of burners in which one or two flat wicks were folded within the wick tube into a cylindrical form. Burners of this sort, many made in Germany, had a built-in centre-draft tube and did not need a special font.

The last major improvement of the Argand burner was patented[20] in 1884 by Leonard Henkle of Rochester, N.Y. The idea is said to have originated with his friend Charles S. Upton of Spencerport, N.Y. Lamps using the Henkle burner became known as Rochester lamps (Fig. 108). The main difference from the traditional Argand burner was the introduction of a cylindrical flame spreader within the central air tube. This spreader was open below, closed on top, and perforated with numerous fine openings on the sides. The effect of this device was to direct a kind of spray of air onto the inner side of the circular flame. This resulted in a distinct improvement in luminosity. Rochester-type burners became almost universal in metal lamps of the late 19th century and reappeared in the Aladdin lamp of the early 20th century.

Maintenance of kerosene lamps was relatively simple as compared with solar lamps, but the daily chore of wick trimming and chimney cleaning, plus periodic refilling of the font, were regular household duties from the 1860s to the 1890s, usually assigned to the younger members of the family. Wicks were trimmed with scissors to remove the charred portions and ragged edges. Fibers projecting from the wick resulted in a smoky flame. For this reason the outer corners of the wick edge were cut at an angle or curve. Later, special wick-trimming shears became available, with a ledge on one blade to catch the cut-off pieces.

In spite of the careful wick trimming and adjusting, some smoke from the flame was inevitable, depositing soot on the inside

Fig. 107. "Student" lamp, Kleeman patent, 1863, 1870. Wolfville Museum, Wolfville, Nova Scotia.

of the glass chimney. This was usually removed by washing with soapy water. A quicker if less effective method was to twist a wad of crumpled newspaper inside the chimney. Special chimney-cleaning devices appeared in the 1860s, with a metal frame that could be expanded inside the chimney to press a piece of cloth against the sooty surface.

The most drastic solution of the smoked-chimney problem was to eliminate it in favor of an extra draft produced by a mechanical fan. The first patent[21] for a kerosene lamp with mechanical draft was issued as early as 1860 to Francis B. De Keravenan of New York, N.Y. In this the base contained a spring motor and a paddle-wheel type fan. The wick

tube was surrounded by a second tube, and the draft from the fan passed up the space between the tubes to the flame. A more practical design appeared in the 1863 patent[22] of George A. Jones of New York. In this the fan is propeller-shaped, and the draft passes up a space between the glass font and an outer metal shell.

The best-known mechanical lamp is that invented and produced by Robert Hitchcock of Watertown, N.Y. He took out a number of patents,[23] beginning in 1872. The typical Hitchcock lamp (Fig. 109) is not much different from the Jones version, except that the font, as well as the outer shell, is of metal.

A mechanical lamp almost identical

Fig. 108. "Rochester" lamp (right), Henkle patent, 1884, and one of its derivatives made by The Miller Co., Meriden, Connecticut, ca. 1895.

Rochester Museum and Science Centre. Photograph courtesy of the Rochester Museum, Rochester, N.Y.

with the Hitchcock was patented[24] in 1887 by Abel G. Heath of New York, N.Y. Heath's Canadian patent of 1886 was assigned to Richard M. Wanzer of Hamilton, Ontario, who manufactured and sold the device as the Wanzer lamp. Although some of these were manufactured in the United States, they were sold only in Canada and Europe, as they might well have been regarded as an infringement of the Hitchcock patents.

Existing Hitchcock and Wanzer lamps, if lubricated, work very well without a chimney. If sluggish, they can be started by blowing upward through the air intake tube.

Illuminating Gas

Gas for lighting purposes was introduced in England in 1799, the invention of the Scottish engineer William Murdoch.[25] It was made by distilling coal at a high temperature. This required an elaborate installation, not only for the generating plant, but also in storage tanks and a complex system of distribution pipes. These essentials restricted illuminating gas to cities and large towns, where it was used mainly in public buildings and for street lighting.

The light from burning gas came from incandescent carbon particles in the flame. Gas burners therefore were designed to produce a wide, flat flame, usually by means of a slit-like opening (Fig. 110). A more effective method appeared in 1820; two small, oblique apertures in the burner tip produced impinging jets of gas, which spread the flame in a high, flat shape. The Argand gas burner, with circular opening and central air duct, was not effective until the appearance of the Welsbach incandescent mantle.

Gas lighting on a commercial scale was introduced in North America in 1816, in

Fig. 109. Mechanical lamp, Hitchcock patent, 1872. National Museum of Man, Ottawa.

Fig. 110. "Fish-tail" gas burners. Mackenzie House, Toronto.

the city of Baltimore, Md. Gas lighting was available in Montreal in 1840 and in Toronto in 1841.

Lighting the gas burner was normally done by holding a burning match over the opening and turning on the stopcock. However, for the elaborate gas fixtures ("gaseliers") from ceilings or for burners high on the wall, a special lighter was required (Fig. 111). This consists of two parallel brass rods or tubes about three feet long, with a wooden handle at one end. At the other end, one rod terminates in a pair of flat fingers, by means of which the stopcock

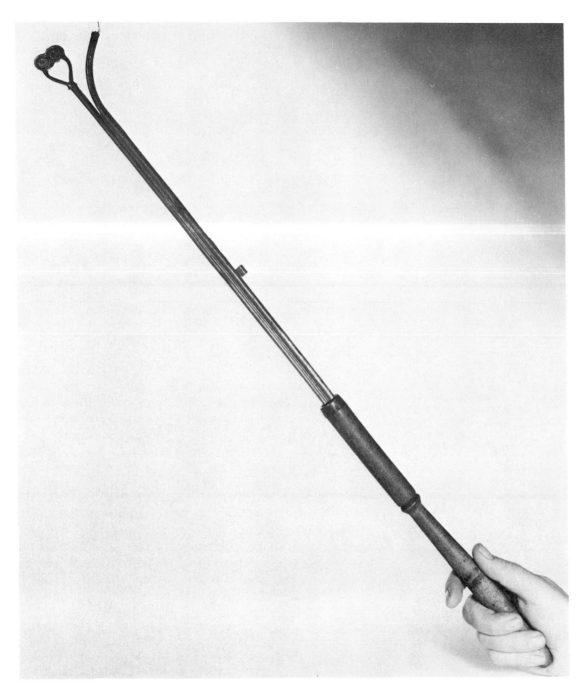

Fig. 111. Gas lighter, LSR Collection. Royal Ontario
Museum photograph.

could be turned. The other rod ends in an
adjustable socket, like a miniature candle
holder, in which a waxed cord or taper was
inserted. The taper was ignited, then used to
light the gas after the stopcock had been
turned.

As gas lighting was being superseded
by kerosene lamps in the late 19th century,
it was given a new if temporary resurgence
by the invention of the incandescent mantle.
Baron Carl Auer von Welsbach, a distin-
guished Austrian chemist, discovered that
fabric impregnated with salts of cerium and
thorium would produce an intense white

light when placed in a gas flame. Although this invention dates from 1885, it was not until 1888 that von Welsbach obtained four U.S. patents,[26] which he assigned to the Welsbach Incandescent Gas Light Co. of New Jersey.

Welsbach mantles (Fig. 112) came as finger-shaped little sacks of soft fabric, which were impregnated with the light-producing salts. The mantle was placed over the aperture of the gas burner and ignited with a match. As the fabric glowed and burned away, it left a fragile skeleton of the impregnating chemicals. The gas was then turned on and lit, and the mantle became white hot and intensely luminous. A mantle would remain effective until broken by a careless touch or the fluttering of a moth, when its remnants would be removed, and the mantle replaced in the usual manner. Gas burners of the mantle era were no longer designed to produce a flat flame; they had

Fig. 112. Wall-mounted gas burner with Welsbach incandescent mantle. LSR Collection.

simple or multiple openings, or the ring-shaped aperture of the Argand burner.

Electric Lighting

The possibility of artificial lighting by means of the electric current had been recognized since 1809, when Sir Humphrey Davy discovered the electric arc. At first the difficulty was to provide an electric current of sufficient power over a long period and at reasonable cost. This was solved in the 1850s with the development of electromechanical generators such as the dynamo. It permitted the use of the electric arc for searchlights, lighthouses, street lamps, and theatrical lighting. But it was much too intense for domestic lighting, and inventors sought a way to "subdivide" the light of the electric arc.

The most promising method seemed to be the use of a conducting wire in a vacuum; passage of an electric current through the wire could heat it to incandescence. Platinum was the substance used in most of the early experiments, but it had too low a melting point. Also, practical means of producing a sufficiently high vacuum were not available at first. This latter problem was solved in the 1870s with the invention of the mercury vacuum pump, usually associated with the name of Hermann Spengler. Coincident with the availability of a device to create a high vacuum, inventors turned to the use of carbon instead of metal as the incandescent conductor.

Early experiments using carbon "filaments" were carried out by J.W. Starr and by W.E. Sawyer and Albon Mann in the United States and by Joseph Swan in England. Each had his own technique for manufacturing a fine carbon conductor suitable for the purpose. Thomas Alva Edison, who did not begin experimenting with carbon filaments until late 1879, solved the problem by charring fine loops of cardboard in an oven. With these as the conductor, and using the mercury vacuum pump, Edison produced a practical electric light[27] by November, 1879. He soon found the card-

Fig. 113. Edison carbon-filament electric light, ca. 1900. LSR Collection.

board filament too fragile, and substituted carbonized bamboo fiber as the conductor. This was not only stronger, but could be made more compact by coiling it into two or more loops. Also, in 1880, Edison produced the familiar "screw-in" type of base (Fig. 113), which has remained, with minor modifications, the standard form to the present.

With the expiration of the basic Edison patents in the 1880s, other inventors entered the race to provide electric lighting. Incandescent electric lights were produced by the Thomson-Houston Company;[28] in these the base had a threaded hole in the center, which screwed onto a threaded post within the socket (Fig. 114). In the Westinghouse light the base had a central pin, which fitted into an opening in the socket.

During the 1890s, electric lighting was mainly used in local installations, such as factories and hotels. One of Edison's first contracts was for electric lighting of the S.S. Columbia. The reason for this situation was that most users of electric lighting had to provide their own generators. For a time there was a great boom in the sale of small electric generating plants. But by 1900 many cities had electric generating and distributing systems, often developed in association with electric street-car companies.

In factories the electric light often hung in a socket from a wire suspended from the ceiling, and was turned on and off by a switch on the wall. This was not appropriate for domestic locations where elaborate lamps and gas fixtures had become normal. So by 1900, electric fixtures resembling those used for gas became popular for the home. In fact, it was common for gas fixtures to be converted to electricity by threading the wires through

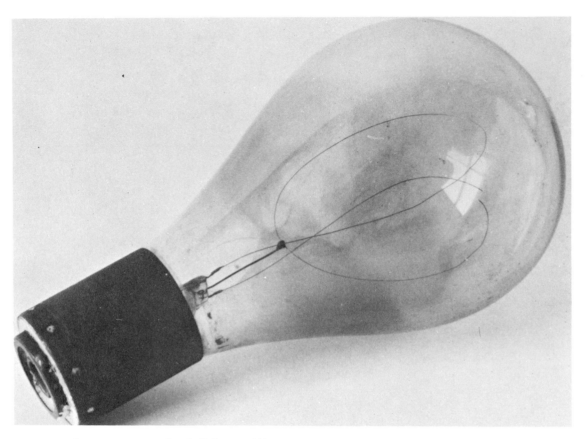

Fig. 114. Thomson-Houston electric light, ca. 1890. LSR Collection.

the gas pipes. Electric fixtures came as ceiling "electroliers" and as wall brackets, convoluted and ornamented like their gas predecessors. There were also electric table lights with flexible cords that could be plugged or screwed into wall outlets. Light sockets with the familiar turn switch ("key"), still in use, were available by 1900.

J.W. Swan of England improved on the carbon light by using a filament made from extruded plastic thread.[29] But by the early 1900s, inventors were returning to metallic filaments using the "rare-earth" metals, such as osmium and tantalum. By 1906, techniques for manufacturing filaments of tungsten were developed.[30] This remained the standard filament for the incandescent electric light for many years. In metal-filament lights the conductor was threaded back and forth in a kind of vertical lattice, suspended from a central glass stem, and to fit this shape the glass bulb was made more nearly cylindrical with only a moderate taper toward the base (Fig. 115).

The success of electric lighting came as much from its convenience as from its luminosity. The gas burner with the Welsbach mantle probably gave more light than the carbon filament, but the electric light required no igniting, but only the flip of a switch. It was cleaner and safer than the gas burner or the oil lamp, and the wires for it could be permanently installed in houses as they were being built.

The invention of the incandescent electric light had a curious sequel that Edison glimpsed dimly. As the basis for the Fleming "valve" and the de Forest "audion" it made practical the wireless telephone and radio broadcasting. By the 1920s, the radio broadcast receiver was an important adjunct to the North American home.

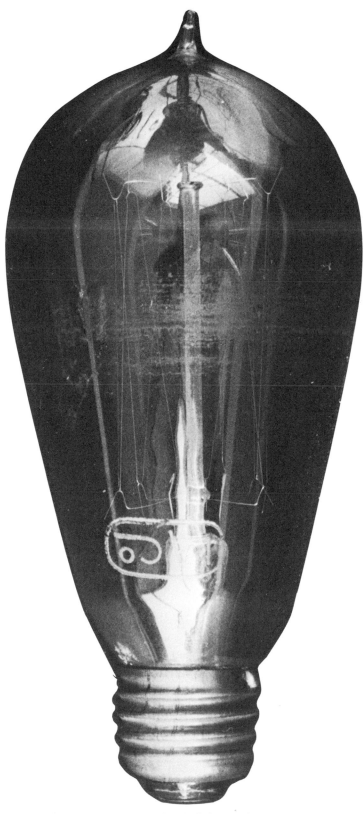

Fig. 115. Tungsten filament electric light, ca. 1911.
LSR Collection.

5 Textiles and Clothing

Spinning and Weaving

The making of textiles by weaving or felting were elaborate operations not usually performed in the home. Weaving, in fact, was a man's trade in the early 19th century, performed by professionals in special quarters, although these might be temporary in the case of the itinerant weaver. Spinning, the making of thread by the twisting of fibers, was in contrast a domestic craft, and was taught to girls at an early age. Skill in spinning was highly esteemed, and is said to have been one of the accomplishments sought by men in seeking a bride.

Well before the end of the 18th century, machines for spinning many threads simultaneously had been developed and set up in factories powered by water wheels. But the domestic spinning wheel persisted, and long after the middle of the 19th century, women in rural North America were preparing wool yarn for knitting or to be taken to the local weaver to be made into blankets or counterpanes. Two very different types of spinning wheels were used. The walking wheel was suitable for wool-spinning only. A typical example had a large wooden wheel with flat rim, which was turned by hand or with a stick from a standing position (Fig. 116). A loop of cord extended from the wheel to a pulley on the spindle mechanism so that moderate speed of the wheel produced rapid rotation of the spindle. This was increased in some models by means of a second set of pulleys, with a short cord drive. The spindle itself was a slender rod of iron, bluntly pointed at the outer end. In spinning, the operator attached a wisp of the carded and greased

wool to the spindle, then gave a flip to the large wheel. As the rotating spindle took up the wool, more was attached, and the operator backed away from the spindle, feeding additional wool onto the rapidly twisting yarn. After several feet had been spun, or the momentum lost, the wheel was given another push, and the formed yarn was allowed to wind into the spindle. The operations were repeated until the spindle was well loaded with yarn, which was then transferred to a reel of some sort. This kind of spinning involved constant walking back and forth, hence the name walking wheel.

In 1856 Lyman Wight of Benton, Pa., patented[1] a wool wheel in which the spindle was mounted on a pendulum arm, which could be swung away or brought back by means of a foot pedal. Thus the operator could be seated, and the effect of walking back and forth was obtained by the movement of the pendulum. In 1867 J.H. Rowe of Hudson, N.Y., patented[2] a similar wheel, but with the spindle arm pivoted from below and moved back and forth by cords attached to the pedal (Fig. 117). This arrangement brought the swinging spindle closer to eye level. A number of the Rowe spinning wheels are preserved in museums in the U.S. and Canada.

The flax wheel is a smaller and more complex device, operated by means of a single or double foot-pedal (Fig. 118). Primarily designed to spin linen thread, it could also be used with wool. The pedal-driven wheel has two channels for the driving cord, which is looped around it twice. One loop goes to the pulley that drives the spindle, the other to a slightly smaller coaxial pulley attached to the take-up bobbin. The spindle, instead of a pointed rod, is a tube, with an opening on the side as well as at the end. Attached just behind this is a horseshoe-shaped wooden

*Fig. 116. "Walking" spinning wheel, for wool yarn.
National Museum of Man, Ottawa.*

device called the flyer, with little hooks along the inner side of each arm. In use, a length of starting yarn was threaded through the spindle and looped through one of the flyer hooks, then secured to the bobbin. The wheel was started revolving and the spinning mechanism began to turn. As the starting yarn twisted, unspun, moistened linen fibers called tow were manipulated onto this yarn and fed into the whirling spindle, acquiring the necessary twist in the process. Because its pulley was smaller than the other, the bobbin revolved a little faster than the spindle, ensuring a tight winding of the new thread as it came off the flyer.

There were various designs of flax wheels. The common type, called the Saxony wheel, has the spindle assembly to the left of the driving wheel. In another, the castle or parlor wheel, the spindle and bobbin were above the drive wheel. Many of these spinning wheels show skillful workmanship and pleasing ornamentation. Flax wheels of metal were also made; they are not as graceful as the wooden wheels, but run smoothly and are easy to operate.

a

b

Fig. 117. Spinning wheel, Rowe patent, 1867: (a) extended position; (b) retracted position. National Museum of Man, Ottawa. Photographs courtesy National Museums of Canada, Ottawa.

a

b

Fig. 118. "Saxony" spinning wheel, for flax and
wool: (a) general view; (b) detail of spindle
and flyer. Black Creek Pioneer Village,
Toronto.

Carpets and Rugs

Floor covers in the early 19th century were usually made of hand-woven fabric, sewn together. Patterns consisted of parallel strips of different colors. Imported carpets with a pile were characteristic of the wealthier households. Small rugs, however, were common, and were made by two methods, braiding and hooking. For braiding rugs it was necessary to prepare narrow strips of cloth by cutting or tearing strips of discarded fabric. Three strips were braided into a rope; by spacing the three strips at different intervals the braid could be continuous. When sufficient length of braid had been prepared, it was sewn together in a circular or oval spiral, producing a more or less flat rug, which could be finished by ironing. Rugs up to three or more feet in diameter were made in this manner. Not much pattern was possible in this method of rug-making, but the medley produced by the random juxtaposition of colors was usually pleasing.

Hooked rugs could be made with rag strips or with heavy yarn. With this technique definite patterns could be created. The base was a piece of burlap or canvas a little larger than the intended rug. This fabric was stretched on a wooden frame. The proposed pattern was sketched on one side with pencil or chalk. The needle was a steel punch, with a small hook at the point (Fig. 119). In making the rug the point of the punch was thrust through the stretched fabric, and a piece of the appropriate rag or yarn was caught below and pulled back through to form a loop of the desired length before being disengaged from the hook. This operation, repeated many times and with suitable selection of colors, produced a layer of loops to form a thick pile. The loops were usually cut to give a softer surface, the underside being secured by sewing on a canvas backing.

A rug pile could be produced much more quickly by means of a device that appeared in the 1860s and is still made for use by hobbyists, under the name of carpet needle (Fig. 120). This instrument consists of two narrow steel bars, one slotted, the other with a screw which slides in the slot. Each bar has a broad wooden handle at one end. At the other end, one bar has a blade-shaped needle with an "eye", the other bar a thin strip of spring steel with a notch at the end. In use, the needle was threaded with the carpet yarn. The two bars were slid on each other so that the needle was thrust through the base fabric, carrying a loop of yarn through the mesh. Without removing the instrument, the position of the two bars was reversed by pushing the other bar down. The notched strip picked off the yarn loop from the needle and prevented it from being pulled out of the fabric. The operation was repeated wherever the pattern called for that color

Fig. 119. Rug hook, modern version of an old device. LSR Collection.

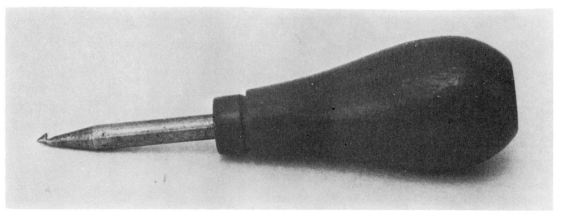

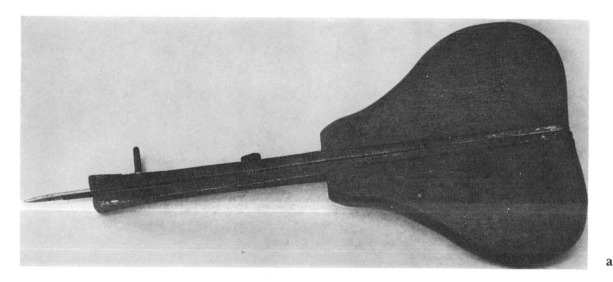

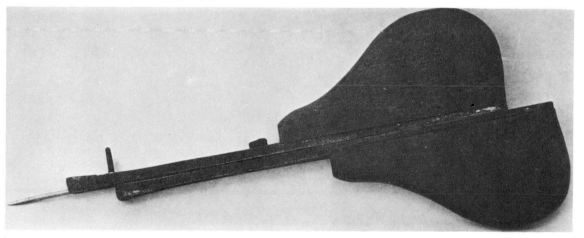

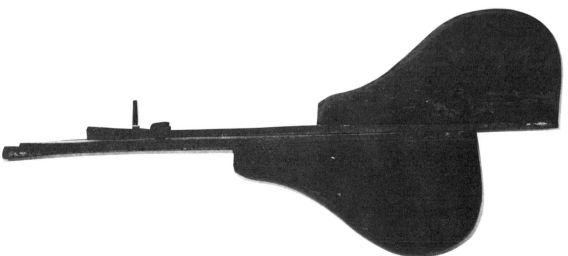

Fig. 120. Carpet needle, Ross patent, 1881: (a) closed;
(b) extended; (c) retracted. LSR Collection.

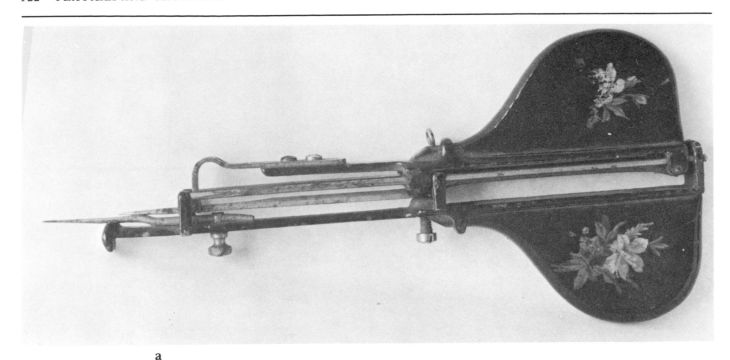

a

b

*Fig. 121. Carpet needle, Weddel patent, 1886:
(a) closed; (b) extended. LSR Collection.*

of yarn. Each loop required only the thrust of the needle bar through the base fabric and withdrawl with the other bar; with practice the operation was rapid.

A number of old as well as modern examples of this carpet needle have survived. The example shown bears the following stamped inscription on the needle handle: **R.W. ROSS/PAT. MAR 6 1882/PAT APR. 8 188(?)**. The first date is that of a Canadian patent[3] issued to Ebenezer Ross, Toledo,

Ohio, for an "Improvement on Machines for Embroidering and Ornamenting Rugs". A U.S. patent[4] for the same invention had been obtained by Ross on December 27, 1881. As described and illustrated, it has the same combination of sliding needle and notched spring strip described above, but the handles are rectangular rather than curved, and there is an attachment for a spool of yarn.

On January 26, 1886, John W. Weddel obtained a U.S. Patent[5] for a "FABRIC-

TURFING IMPLEMENT" (Fig. 121), which involves exactly the same mechanism as the Ross needle, the only important difference being the addition of a forked pressure foot, like that on sewing machines, which can be set to control the depth to which the needle penetrates the fabric. The notched spring that takes off the loop of yarn when the needle is withdrawn slides in a groove on the side of the needle, and its position is adjustable. The example shown is marked in stencilled letters "JEWEL" and bears a fine inscription on the outside of the pressure foot: PAT/JAN/26 86.

In laying a large carpet by tacking it down to the floor, it was necessary to stretch it uniformly, especially if the pattern of strips was to match. To do this by hand pulling was difficult and tiresome, and many mechanical carpet stretchers were devised during the 1850s and later. These usually involved a row of teeth to grip the carpet, and some sort of lever to exert lateral pressure. One of the first, patented[6] in 1853 by J.W. Weatherby, Kingsville, Ohio, had a horizontal rack moved by a pinion, which was turned with a windlass-type lever and locked in position by a pivoted catch (Fig. 122). The carpet was gripped by a cylindrical rod with teeth; this rod could be locked in position by a catch that hooked the end of an arm, and when released, would turn to free the hooks from the carpet. The only awkward thing about this ingenious invention was that it required a board of appropriate length to brace it against the opposite wall.

In stretchers of the Weatherby type the carpet still had to be tacked down with hammer and bruised fingers. Beginning in 1861, combination carpet stretchers and tackers appeared in letters patent. One such that has survived (Fig. 123) was patented[7] in 1865 by B.C. Davis of Herkimer, N.Y. It has the tacking mechanism at the end of an oblique arm of two iron strips, terminating in a wooden handle. At the far end of the arm is a small pivoted plate with four teeth to grip the carpet. The tack driver is a ¼-inch iron rod continuing above into a thicker rod with a broad, flat end. At the lower end of the mechanism is a pair of jaws, which close when the driver is raised

and open when it is depressed. A pivoted arm with notched head serves to feed the tacks from the slot between the two strips of the arm to a position where one can be gripped by the jaws. In use, the slot is loaded with tacks, the carpet pushed to a stretched position, and the driver head struck sharply with a mallet. This forced the jaws open and drove the tack through the carpet into the floor.

Fig. 122. Carpet stretcher, Weatherby patent, 1853.
U.S. Patent drawing.

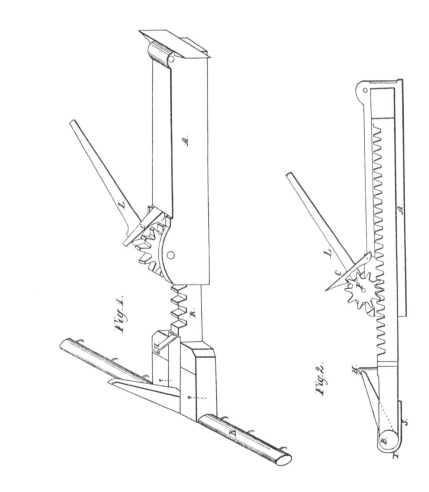

Most carpet stretchers and tackers had to be operated from a kneeling or crouching position. In 1897 a combination device (Fig. 124) was patented[8] by George W. Ansley of Medical Lake and Charles C. May of Davenport, Washington, that could be worked while standing erect. The example shown, which was sold by E.A. Gill & Co. of Toronto under the name of the "Belvidere", differs in some details of the tack-feeding mechanism, but otherwise agrees well with the patent description. The main portion is borne on a wooden shaft, square below, rounded to a handle above. This carries a long, ¼-inch iron rod terminating in a push-knob above, and threaded through four screw-eyes. The lower end of the rod passes into a funnel-shaped aperture, and out through a pointed opening otherwise closed by a spring strip. A short, narrow board is attached to the main shaft by two metal-strip pivots and terminates with a notched iron plate with eight hook-shaped teeth. On the main shaft, adjacent to the driver rod, is a slotted receptacle for the tacks.

In use the device was placed with the short board on the carpet, with the toothed end near but not at the edge of the area to be tacked. The main shaft was inclined a little towards the operator, who placed one foot on the board and pushed the handle forward. This engaged the carpet with the teeth, and pushed it ahead. The operation could be repeated until the desired tension was obtained. Then the driving rod was pulled up about a foot to release a tack into the funnel, then driven downward to hammer the tack into the floor. As noted, the 1897 patent shows a more complex tack-feeding mechanism, but the one in the example described works very well.

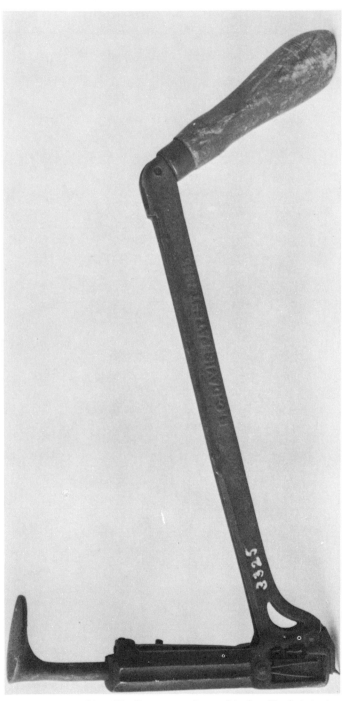

Fig. 123. Carpet stretcher and tacker, Davis patent, 1865. LSR Collection.

Sewing

The sewing of leather or cloth to make or repair clothing has been a domestic craft for thousands of years. By the late 18th century the skillful seamstress was highly esteemed, and art forms such as embroidery and quilting permitted some individual expression. Nevertheless, hand sewing was one of the more tedious of domestic tasks. Early in

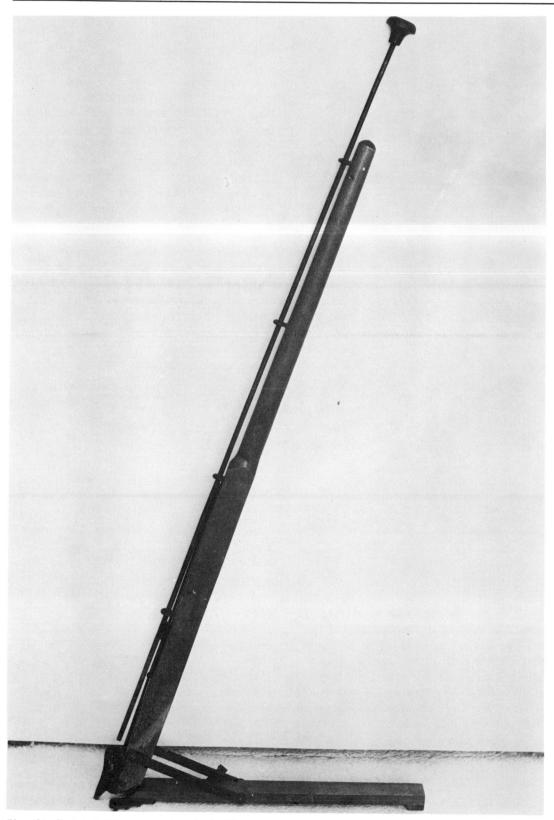

*Fig. 124. Carpet stretcher and tacker, Ansley-May
    patent, 1897. LSR Collection.*

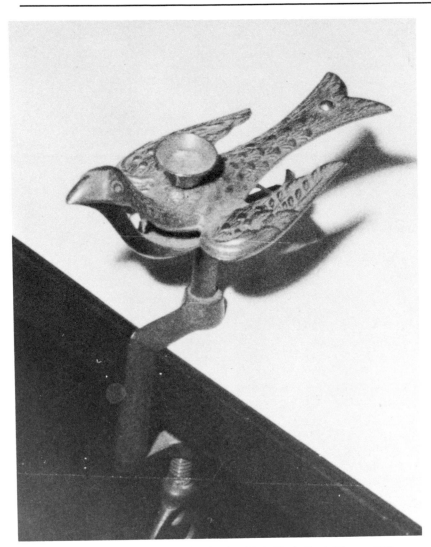

Fig. 125. Sewing bird, Black Creek Pioneer Village, Toronto.

pin-cushions to hold the needles when not in use. A kind of third hand was provided by means of a spring clamp to hold the seam while it was sewn. By the 19th century this had evolved into the sewing bird, a sheet-metal device shaped like a bird poised for flight (Fig. 125). It was attached to a table edge by means of a screw clamp. Pressing down on the tail caused the spring-loaded beak to open; releasing allowed the beak to close and act as a clamp. Sewing birds were elaborated by various additions, such as measuring tape in the 1854 patent[9] of Julius E. Merriman of Meriden, Conn.

Sewing Machines

The fascinating story of the invention and development of the sewing machine has been told in detail (Cooper, 1966; Ewer and Baylor, 1970). It is a tale of ingenious mechanisms, struggling inventors, and industrial rivalries and combinations. Most of the events occurred in the United States, but the product, and to some extent the production, spilled over into Canada.

Sewing machines may be classified on the basis of the kind of stitch that they produce. Broadly speaking, these are: the running stitch, with a single thread; the chain stitch, with one or two threads; the lock stitch, using two threads. It is convenient, if not historically sequential, to describe the early sewing machines under these three categories.

The running stitch is a simple under-and-over operation, used mainly for basting prior to final sewing. It is not a tight stitch, and can be pulled out easily. Nevertheless, the first sewing machine patented[10] in the United States, by John J. Greenough in 1842, used this stitch. The needle was double-pointed, with the eye in the middle, and was passed back and forth through the cloth by two pincer-like devices, one on each side. Apparently it was never manufactured commercially.

In basting by hand it is common practice to fold the two cloth edges a number of times, then pass the needle and thread through all the folds at once. This technique

the 19th century a demand for mass-produced garments developed, and factories grew up in which numerous women were employed. Hours were long, pay was small, and working conditions were bad. The creation of a mechanical device for sewing was looked upon not only as a contribution to industry, but also as a humanitarian means of freeing women from the tiring and eye-straining labor of sewing by hand. Unfortunately, as sewing machines became practical and available, they made possible an even greater exploitation of female labor.

Before the advent of the sewing machine, a few simple aids were available. There were

was used in the basting machine patented[11] by Benjamin W. Bean in 1843. It had a system of interlocking gears through which the two cloth edges were fed. The gears threw the cloth into folds, which were impaled by a curved needle carrying the thread. This type of machine had only moderate use, but it reappeared in a patent[12] by Aaron Palmer in 1863. The Palmer (Fig. 126) version was smaller and simpler than the original Bean model, and used a conventional straight needle. It was entirely of metal. Sold under the name of Fairy Sewing Machine, it had a brief popularity, and a number of examples are preserved in museums.

The chain stitch is usually made with a single thread, but a double chain can be made with two threads. In chain stitching a loop is made by passing the needle and thread through the cloth then withdrawing the needle but leaving the loop of thread on

the underside. A second loop is formed, the thread being passed through the first loop. Continuation of the process forms a seam that is strong and tight, but because each loop is dependent for security on the following loop, the whole chain can be unraveled by pulling on the thread at the last loop. This can be secured by a knot, but a break in the stitching can also lead to unraveling. For this reason sewing machines using the chain stitch did not become popular for sewing clothes, but were, and still are, widely used in industry, as for example in the making of cloth bags for vegetables, sugar, or flour.

The first sewing machine to use the chain stitch was the invention of Bartholemy Thimonnier of Paris, who obtained a French patent in 1830 and a U.S. patent[13] in 1850. His machine used a hooked needle to form the loop. Due to the opposition of French

Fig. 126. Running-stitch sewing machine, Palmer patent, 1863. National Museum of Man, Ottawa.

tailors, the Thimonnier machine was not a commercial success. A machine using a needle with the eye near the point was patented[14] by Charles Morey and Joseph B. Johnson in 1849. The most practical of chain-stitch machines was that of James E.A. Gibbs, patented[15] in 1856. This had a "looper-hook" to hold the thread loop open for the next loop to pass through. The Gibbs machine, manufactured by the Willcox & Gibbs Sewing Machine Co., had some popularity at first as a domestic appliance, due to its relatively low price, but as lock-stitch machines became cheaper, it found its main market with industry, and machines not much different from the early Gibbs models continued to be made for industrial use well into the 20th century (Fig. 127).

In the double-loop chain stitch two threads are used. One is thrust through the cloth by a needle, in the usual manner, to form a loop below the platform. The second or locking thread is pushed through this loop as a loop of its own. The needle is then withdrawn, leaving its loop secured by the loop of the locking thread. On the next down stroke the needle thrusts a second loop through the horizontal loop of the shuttle thread, thus locking that loop. A second shuttle-thread is thrust through the second needle loop and the operation is repeated. Unlike that of the single-loop stitch, the seam

Fig. 127. Sewing machine, Willcox & Gibbs patent, 1856. LSR Collection.

so formed is secure. A machine using the double-loop stitch was patented[16] by William O. Grover and William E. Baker in 1851. Because it used twice as much thread as a single-loop machine, the Grover and Baker machine did not become popular, but in later years its principle became the basis of high-speed industrial sewing machines, partly because it used continuous threads.

The lock stitch is not one ordinarily used in hand sewing, and its introduction was a drastic break from traditional techniques. Two threads are required, one to form a loop, as in the chain stitch, the other to pass through the loop and so lock it. This is the basic stitch of nearly all the successful sewing machines of the 19th century. Apparently the first machine to use it was built by Walter Hunt of New York about 1832; in this the loop was formed by an eye pointed needle, and the lock by a miniature oscillating shuttle. The Hunt invention was not patented and was never produced commercially. In 1839 an Austrian inventor Josef Madersperger, patented a machine using a form of lock stitch.

The sewing machine industry is generally regarded as dating from the invention of Elias Howe, Jr., of Cambridge, Mass., who obtained a patent[17] in 1846. In the Howe machine the slightly curved, eye-pointed needle is swung in a vertical arc on a pendulum-like arm (Fig. 128). The two layers of cloth being sewn together are held vertically by a series of sharp pins projecting from a metal "baster-plate". Each stroke of the needle through the cloth forms a loop of thread on the other side. A miniature shuttle with a tiny bobbin of thread is impelled back and forth on a raceway by two arms. It is passed through the needle loop, then the needle is withdrawn, and the shuttle returns to the starting position. With each stitch the baster plate moves the cloth into position for the next one.

Howe endured years of poverty, discouragement and tragedy in the United States and England while attempting to obtain support for the manufacture of his machine. Success came to him through the incorporation of his invention in machines devised and built by others. Howe sued for

Fig. 128. Sewing machine, Howe patent model, 1846. U.S. National Museum of History and Technology. Smithsonian Institution photograph.

patent infringement and eventually won. Although a gentle and tolerant man, he exacted a heavy toll of licence fees to compensate for his early struggles.

Machines bearing the name "Howe" came on the market in the late 1850s. Most of these were manufactured by his brother, Amasa B. Howe. They were unlike the original Howe design, using a straight vertical needle and incorporating the devices of other patents. Howe machines made by his sons-in-law, the Stockwell brothers, appeared in the 1870s and 1880s. Many other makes bear the name Howe on the name plate to indicate that the manufacturer had paid the required licence fee.

Many important improvements on the

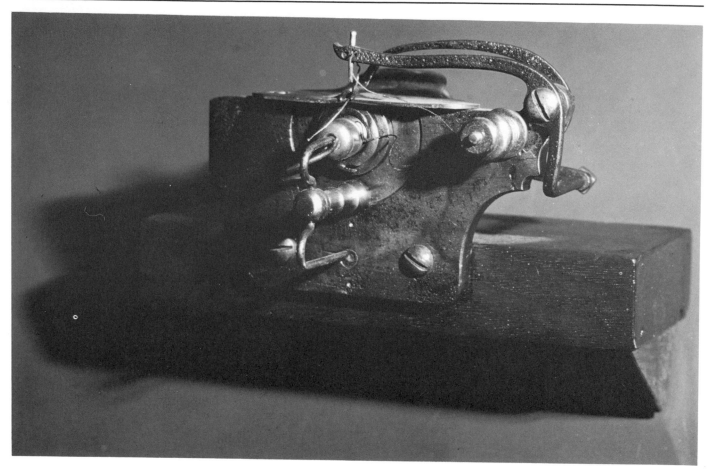

Fig. 129. Sewing machine, Wilson patent model, 1851. U.S. National Museum of History and Technology, Washington, D.C.

Howe machine were made by Allan B. Wilson of Watertown, Conn. His first patent[18] in 1850 used a straight vertical needle, and a double-pointed shuttle to form a lock on both strokes. The cloth was moved on a sliding bar, as in the Howe machine. In 1851[19] Wilson substituted a rotary hook for the shuttle and a stationary bobbin (Fig. 129). The following year he introduced[20] the four-motion cloth feed, in which a movable block in the platform carried the cloth forward, then dropped clear and moved back for the next advance. The combination of this with the stationary bobbin was the basis of the highly successful domestic sewing machines manufactured and sold by the Wheeler, Wilson Co. of Bridgeport, Conn. (Fig. 130).

By the late 1880s the name Singer was almost synonymous with sewing machine, but its fame rested as much on excellent manufacture and vigorous marketing as on original invention. Isaac Merritt Singer of New York City took out his first sewing-machine patent[21] in 1851. This was followed by 21 more patents, the last[22] in 1867. Singer's original contributions included the streamlined shuttle actuated by a swinging arm, the yielding pressure foot to hold down the cloth during the withdrawl of the needle (Fig. 131), and the double-action foot pedal. He incorporated the eye-pointed needle and reciprocating shuttle of Howe and the four-motion feed of Wilson. This brought him into a prolonged legal battle with Elias Howe, which he eventually lost. After this the principal sewing-machine manufacturers agreed to pool their existing patents, each participant receiving a stipulated share of the general profits, and all paying a licence fee to Howe. Although the "Combination" worked well for existing companies, it made it difficult for new companies to make a start. Some avoided the problem by setting up manufacturing in Canada, ostensibly for the Canadian market, but no doubt having some of their products taken illegally into the United States.

Canadian patents for lock-stitch and chain-stitch machines were issued in 1854 and 1860, but there is no evidence that they were offered for sale. In 1861 Frederick Rogers

of Hamilton, Ontario, obtained a patent[23] for a double-loop machine, ten years after the Grover and Baker patent. The Rogers machine was offered for sale in Hamilton in 1861.

Wheeler and Wilson sewing machines were offered for sale in Canada in 1855,[24] and were being made under licence in Kingston in 1859.[25] In 1860 a Canadian sewing-machine industry began with the establishment of a factory in Hamilton,

Fig. 130. Sewing machine, Wheeler & Wilson, ca. 1860. Black Creek Pioneer Village, Toronto.

Fig. 131. Sewing machine, Singer patent model, 1851. U.S. National Museum of History and Technology. Smithsonian Institution photograph.

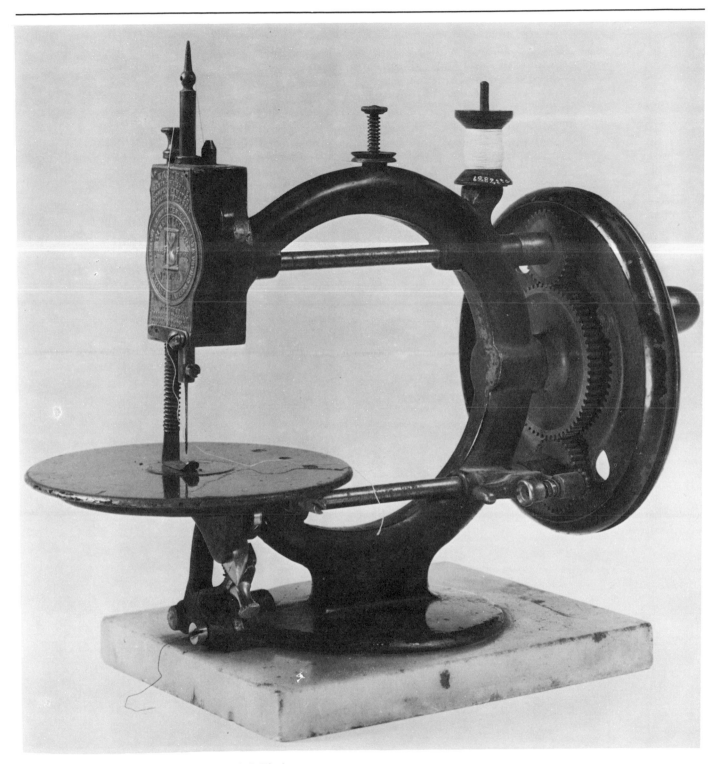

Fig. 132. Sewing machine, Wanzer patent, 1867. Black Creek Pioneer Village, Toronto. Royal Ontario Museum photograph.

Ontario, by Richard Mott Wanzer, formerly of Buffalo, N.Y.[26] The Wanzer machine combined the main elements of the Wheeler and Wilson machine with the reciprocating shuttle of Singer (Fig. 132). Wanzer machines were not sold in the United States, but had a flourishing sale in the 1860s and 1870s, not only in Canada, but also in Britain, France, South Africa, Australia, Brazil, and Japan. Later Wanzer machines included both table and floor-stand, pedal-operated models. By the late 1880s, however, competition from U.S. manufacturers began to hurt, and the production of the Wanzer sewing machine ceased in 1890.

The other principal manufacturer of sewing machines in Canada was Charles Raymond, of Guelph, Ontario. Raymond was also an American, who took out a U.S. patent[27] for a chain-stitch machine in 1858 and set up a factory with W.H. Nettleton in Brattleboro, Vermont. In 1862 he moved to Guelph and began manufacturing sewing machines under his U.S. patents,[28] 1858 to 1861 (Fig. 133). In 1872 he took out a Canadian patent[29] for a lock-stitch machine,

Fig. 133. Sewing machine, Raymond patent, 1858. National Museum of Man, Ottawa.

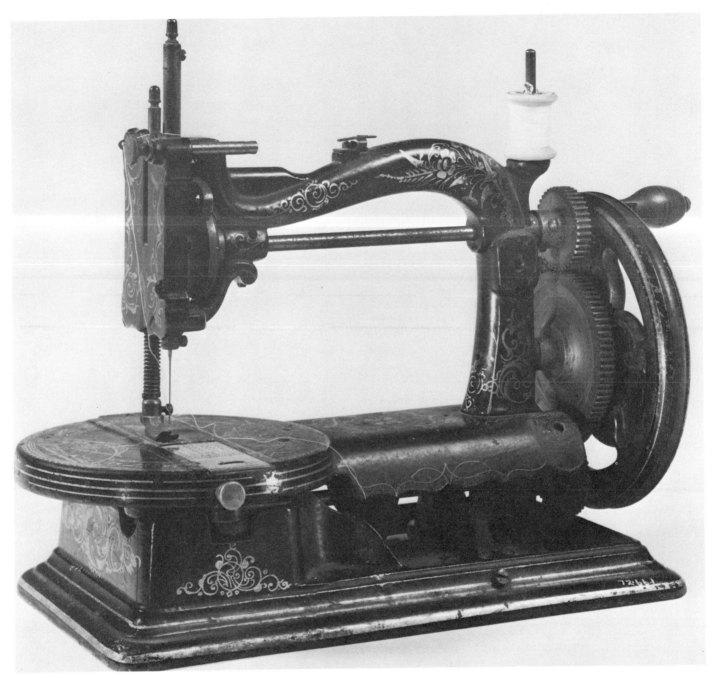

Fig. 134. Sewing machine, Raymond patent, 1872.
Black Creek Pioneer Village, Toronto.
Royal Ontario Museum photograph.

having a horizontal shuttle and a four-motion feed plate (Fig. 134). Raymond machines were made in Guelph for the remainder of the century but the company was eventually taken over by the White Sewing Machine Co. of Cleveland, Ohio.

6 *Next to Godliness*

Many domestic activities had their own satisfaction of accomplishment: a sumptuous meal prepared and enjoyed, a handsome dress sewn and worn, happy and healthy children cared for. But the daily battle against dust and grime, involving not only the physical components of the home but also its inhabitants, was a struggle in which the brief satisfaction of accomplishment was diluted by the certainty that it would all have to be done again in a day or week. Any success of technology in reducing the exertion and the drudgery of cleaning was a step towards that happy day when almost any home could have a host of servants, the many mechancial and electrical devices that have made 20th century living unique in world history.

Floor Cleaning

Sweeping the floor with a broom is perhaps the oldest form of house cleaning, going back even to the earthen floors of primitive societies. The North American home of the early 19th century had available a variety of brooms. The simplest, and perhaps the earliest in the pioneer home was made by tying together a small bundle of slender twigs. The result was more of a brush than a broom, but it was adequate for sweeping ashes back into the fireplace, and for roughly cleaning a split-log floor.

The birch broom was a true broom, complete with handle. It was one of the things Indian craftsmen made to sell in the white settlements. A pole of birch or other straight-grained wood was whittled down part way to form a number of narrow strips still attached to the stem. These were then bent outward and downward, and their upper, bent edges were tied against the uncut portion of the pole inside the cluster. The bundle of strips formed the strands of the

Fig. 135. Straw broom, made on original broom machine, Black Creek Pioneer Village, Toronto.

broom, and the partly peeled pole was the handle. It was a better broom than the bundle of twigs, but still not very effective. An old saying described unkempt hair as looking like a birch broom in the fits.

Corn straw was the favorite material for making brooms, and a special variety is still used for this purpose. A bundle of strands could be bound on a pole by hand, but there was also a machine for doing this, insuring a firm packing and secure binding. Brooms made in this manner were excellent, but their narrow, cylindrical form does not cover much area with one sweep (Fig. 135).

The modern wide, flat broom was in use by the 1850s, for in 1852 a U.S. patent[1] was issued to Cyrus T. Moore of Concord, New Hampshire, for an improvement in this type of broom, which involved holding the straw by a clasp, with an attachment for the handle. Normally, the straw was packed in a jig and sewn together by hand. This type of broom was reserved for use on carpets and on the better floors, and the birch or twig broom was used at the fireplace, or in the cellar or the kithcen shed.

The broom was not a satisfactory means of cleaning carpets, and if these were removable they were hung on a clothesline or a horizontal pole and beaten to dislodge the dirt. Any kind of a paddle would do, but a special beater made from a loop of stringy wood or cane was preferred. A more sophisticated version had the ends secured in a handle. Later a wire loop was substituted for that of cane (Fig. 136). Beating was hard on the carpet and tiring for the beater. Besides, it was not practical with carpets fastened to the floor. In 1858 mechanical carpet sweepers made their appearance, six patents being granted in that year by the U.S. Patent Office. The first[2] chronologically is that issued to Hiram H. Herrick of East Boston, Mass. Like most of the sweepers that followed, the Herrick device (Fig. 137) consisted of a low box, open on the underside, cog-like driving wheels, and a shaft having rows of brushes, which was rotated by the driving wheels in direction opposite to that of the drive wheels. As the sweeper was pushed over the carpet, the dust was swept up by the brushes, the coarser particles being

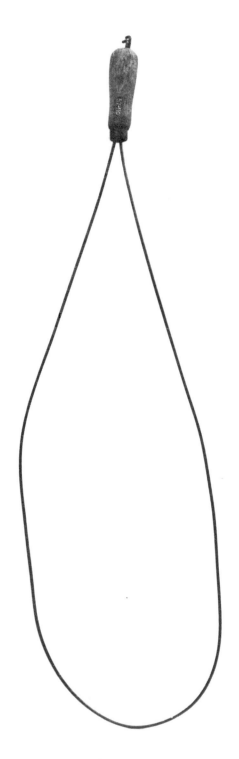

Fig. 136. Wire carpet beater, Black Creek Pioneer Village, Toronto.

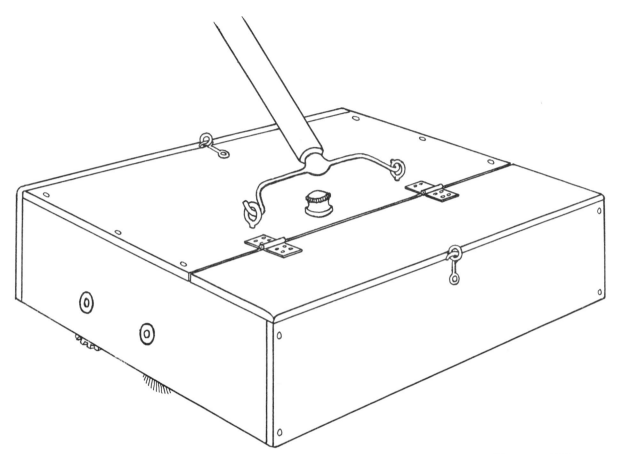

*Fig. 137. Carpet sweeper, Herrick patent, 1858.
Drawing by LSR, based on the patent
drawings.*

deposited in a receptacle at the front of the sweeper, the finer material in a trough at the rear. Like most of the early sweepers, the Herrick model could sweep only in one direction.

The modern carpet sweeper dates from 1876, when Melville R. Bissell of Grand Rapids, Michigan, obtained a patent[3] for a sweeper in which the brush shaft was driven by two cog wheels located at mid-width, and arranged so that they operated the brushes in both forward and backward motion. Support for the sweeper was provided by four small bearing wheels at the corners. The success of the Bissell carpet sweeper was due not only to the excellence of design, but also

to the business ability of Mr. and Mrs. Bissell and their sales methods.[4] By the end of the 19th century the name Bissell was almost synonymous with carpet sweeper. Four models are illustrated in the Sears, Roebuck catalogue of 1896 (Fig. 138). Even today the Bissell sweeper of Grand Rapids has a world-wide distribution and a well-deserved popularity.

Although the carpet sweeper has remained an important aid to floor cleaning, it has long been surpassed in effectiveness by the vacuum cleaner. But this was a device that had to wait for the perfection of small electric motors. Suction cleaners using large pumps were in use in the 1890s, but mostly

SEARS, ROEBUCK & CO., (Incorporated), Cheapest Supply House on Earth, Chicago.   103

WRINGERS.

Our Wringers are manufactured by a firm who have been in this business for thirty years. The workmanship is of the highest order. All parts are closely matched, with no rough, ragged or chipped edges. Even the under parts and inside of posts are finished smoothly. The rubber rolls are the vital part of the machine. The warranted rolls in our Wringer are made of **solid white rubber** and they are vulcanized immovably to the shaft. **We guarantee that should any warranted rolls turn on the shaft, become loose, bulge or give out because of defects within a year from time of being put into service, we will replace them free of charge.**
Wringers weigh about 10 lbs. each.

No. 15364. The Cyclone iron frame Wringer, with steel springs, galvanized malleable iron apron. Rolls, 10x1¾ inches. This wringer will give satisfaction for the price, and we have never seen its equal sold at anything like this price. Only $1.30.

No. 15367. The Cleveland Ball Bearing **Wringer.** The greatest improvement yet applied to clothes wringers. Turns with half the strength required for others. This **ball** bearing must not be confounded with the roller bearing introduced some years ago. The arrangement of this bearing is almost identically the same as applied to bicycles. The cones and bearings are made of steel, hardened and tempered, and the balls of hardened steel, same as are used in bicycles. Has wood frame, steel adjusting spring, 2 adjusting screws; rolls, 10x1¾ inches; **warranted.** Price, each, $3.20.

No. 15368. The Peerless Wringer is the most popular wringer with high-class trade, and we can not recommend it too highly. The distinguishing feature of the Peerless is the clamping device which has recently been imitated by other makers, but comparison shows the imitation is only in general appearance and not in fine workmanship and finish which characterizes the Peerless. Has guide roller, double gears and rolls 10x1¾ inches; warranted. Price, each, $2.

No. 15369. The Unrivaled Wringer. Desiring to give our customers a large variety of wringers to select from we have added this first-class Wringer to our line. The material for the frame is carefully selected from first-class lumber. Has guide roller, 2 top screws and swinging iron clamps. Rolls, 10x1¾ inches; **warranted.** Price, each, $2.

No. 15372. The Perfection Wringer. While this Wringer will give excellent satisfaction for the price, and is as good as the first quality of some makers, the frame is not made from the same **selected** material as our other wood frame wringers. The frame is good and strong and the rolls of good material. Size, 10x1¾ inches; not warranted. Price, each, $1.50.

No. 15375. The combination of Wringer and Bench combined is popular, and the Peerless is the best in the market. The bench is constructed on the principle of the truss bridge, and is exceedingly strong, though light. When folded for shipment or putting away when not in use it occupies but little space. With the ordinary tub wringer it is about as much work to hold the tub as to turn the wringer. The Bench Wringer does away with all this trouble. Rolls, 10x1¾ inches; warranted. Price, each, $3.50.

When you build your house, barn, or other buildings, buy your hardware and material of us, and save enough to pay your carpenter bill.

CARPET SWEEPERS.
Something New. Cheap as a Broom.

No. 15379. Bissell's Baby Sweeper is a toy that every parent will want. It is useful, durable, beautiful and cheap. The maker's name is a guarantee that it is first class in material and workmanship. Is about quarter the size of a regular sweeper, has broom action, strongly made and nicely finished. Price, each, 42c.

No. 15380. Bissell's Child Sweeper is a toy or a light small sweeper for practical use. Is about ½ size of a regular sweeper, has broom action. Price, each, 75c.
Our Carpet Sweepers are not mere crumb brushes. They do away entirely with the need of a broom on the carpet. They go into the nap and raise the dirt from where the broom never reaches. They will follow up a broom and remove more dirt than the broom did.
They sweep without dust or noise or wear on the carpet—almost without labor. They sweep any carpet.
The largest sweeper makers in the world make them. Sixty-five patents cover their devices.
And the price is low. Quantity makes it low.

No. 15382. The Sears, Roebuck & Co.'s Sweeper is unquestionably the best low priced sweeper ever put on the market. It is a good sweeper and a good looker. It has the broom action—everlasting pure bristle brush—and spring dumping device.
The case is made with selected 3-ply veneer top, gracefully curved and attractively finished. Price, each, $1.95.

No. 15384. Bissell's "Grand Rapids." The best known and most widely sold carpet sweeper in the world.
Contains the famous Bissell broom action and every other patented feature necessary in a first class sweeper.
Made from the best selected cabinet woods in an assortment of attractive finishes.
Has rubber furniture protector encircling the case, Bissell's patented reversible bail-spring, wheels outside the case, our everlasting pure bristle brush, both pans open at once by an easy pressure of the finger. Weight, 6 lbs. Price, each, $2.35.

If you don't find just what you want quoted, write for prices. We can supply you with anything in the Hardware line, and always at lowest factory prices.

Fig. 138. *Clothes wringers and carpet sweepers, Sears, Roebuck and Co. catalogue, 1896.*

Reproduction courtesy Sears, Roebuck and Co.

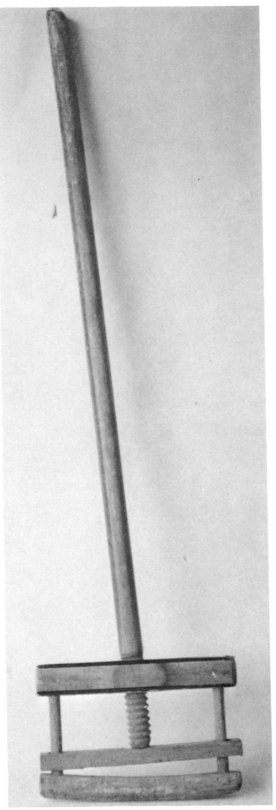

Fig. 139. Wooden mop head, Black Creek Pioneer Village, Toronto.

for major cleaning operations, as in hotels and theatres. Small hand-operated, piston-type suction cleaners also appeared about this time. But vacuum cleaners as such were not listed among U.S. patents until 1909, when a number suddenly appeared. Lifshey[4] has given a graphic account of the development of the vacuum cleaner, but most of this occurred in the 20th century.

Sooner or later floors had to be washed, and this was usually done by scrubbing with a stiff brush and wiping with a large cloth. Performed in a kneeling position, it was another of the more exhausting household labors. The cloth, saturated with dirty water, had to be wrung out by hand. A somewhat easier method was to use a mop, a bundle of cloths or cords tied around the end of a pole. Even this, however, required hand-wringing of the mop head.

In the 1850s a number of U.S. patents for mop heads were issued. These had bars that formed a kind of vice for the mop cloth, which was secured by turning the handle. Most of these mop-heads were of metal, but wooden versions also were used, some of them home-made (Fig. 139). Mechanical mop wringers also were devised, similar to clothes wringers, and mounted on the rim of the pail.

Vermin Traps

Household vermin have been problems for centuries, especially for city dwellers. For a long time the main defense was provided by dogs and cats. By the 18th century, rat traps using a spring-loaded jaw and a baited trigger were in use, often set out by a professional exterminator. Rats seem to have been regarded as the most serious household menace. As early as 1838 a U.S. patent[5] was issued to T. Kell of Alexandria, Va., for an improved rat trap. It was not until 1869 that the first U.S. patent[6] was issued for a mouse trap, to A.G. Davis of Watertown, Conn. Most traps were based on the principle of spring-loaded jaws (Fig. 140). Some people, however, objected to removing the carcass from the trap; it might be bloody or putrescent, or

Fig. 140. Mouse trap, multiple, Black Creek Pioneer Village, Toronto.

bearing lice. So live traps were devised, in which the animal was lured by means of bait, and the entrance closed by the release of a trigger (Fig. 141). The captured animal could then be drowned by submerging the trap in a pail of water.

The menace of the house fly was not fully appreciated until the discovery of disease-producing bacteria and the ways in which these could be spread. But people evidently found the presence of flies unpleasant because of their association with decaying food and garbage. The first mechanical fly trap to be patented[7] in the U.S. was devised by J.B. Fuller and G.W. Pierce of Worchester, Mass., 1850. In this the flies were lured onto a baited wheel or belt and carried into a receptacle.

The most detested domestic insect pest was the bed-bug, not only because of its association with dirt, but because it sucked blood from its sleeping victims. The remedy most widely recommended was cleanliness of house and bedding, but professional exterminators used chemicals or steam. A bed-bug trap was patented in 1829 by J.A. Clark of Georgetown, D.C. It was not until 1865 that a similar patent[8] was issued, to W.

Fig. 141. Mouse trap, cage type, Black Creek Pioneer Village, Toronto.

Tapper of New York, N.Y. His device consisted of a braided frame at one end of the bed which entrapped the pests, and from which they could be shaken out and destroyed.

Laundry

The technique of removing dirt from clothing and bedding involves two operations: mechancial circulation of water through the textile, and solution of the grease by means of soap or detergent. In many countries the washing of clothes involves only the first of these actions. The fabrics are rubbed and beaten, and repeatedly rinsed in water, usually at the edge of a stream. In western Europe and North America, some form of soap has been used for centuries. Soap is a compound of sodium or potassium with the fatty acids (e.g., potassium stearate, etc.). In pre-industrial days soap was made in the home by boiling animal fat in a strong solution of potash (potassium hydroxide), skimming off the floating product, and allowing it to harden. Often such soap contained excess potash, which could damage clothes during washing. About the middle of the 19th century, soap made under controlled conditions, and using sodium hydroxide as the alkali, became available for purchase, but in rural areas the making of soap at home continued for many years, using waste grease from the kitchen and "lye" purchased in cans at the store.

In spite of soap and other aids, washing was an arduous task, involving repeated rubbing and squeezing, first in the soap

Fig. 146. Connor washing machine, Raulston patent, 1884. National Museum of Man, Ottawa.

machine of today still uses this same reciprocating rotation of the agitator.

After the clothes had been washed and rinsed, they were "wrung out" to remove the excess water. The old way was twisting the wet clothes by hand, and this action was simulated in the mechanical wringer patented[18] in 1847 by Ira Avery of Tunkhan-nock, Pa. In this the wet clothes were placed in a sack, which was attached at the ends to clamps at either end of a narrow tub. One of these clamps was turned by means of a crank, twisting the sack and its contents to expel most of the water.

The clothes wringer consisting of two rollers, like those of the roller washing

SEARS, ROEBUCK & CO., (Incorporated), Cheapest Supply House on Earth, Chicago.   107

No. 15620. Our Own Folding Ironing Board, has a steel wire tension at the bottom, which acts as an automatic folder; when set upright it can be used as a step ladder; in operating it, all you have to do is to open up the legs, then press upon the large end of the board. Give it a trial and you will have no other, as it certainly is the most complete table in use; weight, 18 lbs. Price, each, $1.

No. 15621. The Champion Bosom Board and Stretcher; the most complete in the market. After you have once used this board you will never be without one. Price, 40c.

EUREKA ADJUSTABLE CLOTHES BAR.

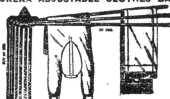

No. 15623. Eureka Adjustable Clothes Bar, intended to fasten to the wall. When not in use takes the space of an ordinary broom. The bars are 3 feet in length, with gilt tips; a very convenient household article; weight, 4 lbs. Each, 39c.
No. 15624. Same as No. 15623, with 6 bars, 2 feet long. Each, 25c.

No. 15625. The Excelsior Clothes Dryer; is made of picked ash bars 1¼ of an inch thick, folds up snug against the wall when not in use, takes up less space and has more capacity than any other bar made; 10 bars, 36 inches long, each, 30c; 6 bars, 24 inches, each, 27c.

SCHMUCK'S MOP WRINGER.

No. 15626. Schmuck's Mop Wringers for simplicity, durability, dry wringing and adaptability have no equal. They are manufactured of wrought iron, the rollers made of hard maple chemically treated, and will fit any size pail. It is self-wringing, and while mopping, gloves can be used, as the hands do not come in contact with water; in fact, what has heretofore proven the dirtiest work in and about a house is now made the easiest and cleanest by the use of this mop wringer. Price for wringer with pail each, $2.25.

No. 15627. The Globe Perfect Self-Wringing Mop. The mop is made of cotton coils, large and full size. We believe this to be the most acceptable and best wearing wringing mop ever offered for sale. Each, 25c.

We list a very fine line of Men's Laundered and Unlaundered Shirts. Refer to the department of Gents' Furnishings.

S., R. & CO. IMPROVED WESTERN STAR WASHING MACHINE. NO. 2 "FAMILY SIZE."

No. 15630. The Western Star Washer is acknowledged by all to be the best and most perfect machine on the market. No nails or iron of any kind are used in its construction which can come in contact with the clothes, causing iron rust on the linen, as is the case with other machines; this, together with other improvements, that have been made in this machine and not contained in any other, are of the greatest importance and must be seen to be appreciated. If you desire a more complete description of this machine send for descriptive circular, which will be mailed on application. Weight, 65 lbs. Price, $3.50.

ANTHONY WAYNE WASHER. NO. 2 "FAMILY SIZE."

No. 15633. The Anthony Wayne Washer, with corrugated stave and bottom. This is the best round washer made. Some prefer the round washer to the square; we have selected the Anthony Wayne as being the best on the market, and we offer it at a price which places it within the reach of all. Weight, 50 lbs. Price, $2.50.

CLINE'S IMPROVED STEAM WASHER.

No. 15635. Cline's Improved Steam Washer has several new features that others do not have. Has a corrugated cylinder, sliding cover and a faucet attached to the boiler for removing the water without lifting the boiler from the stove, which is a decided advantage. Weight, 32 lbs. Price, each, $6.

RACINE HOUSEHOLD MANGLES.

It is a well known fact that clothes are kept in a more healthful condition and will wear much longer when mangled than when hot irons are used.

No. 15638. This mangle is designed for small families, and particularly where economy in room is to be considered. It is made sufficiently strong to sustain the necessary pressure to do good work. It is light and easily handled and takes up about the same space as a wringer. It is constructed on the same principle as the large size machines, with strong coil springs at the ends of the rolls, the pressure being adjusted by the thumb screws. The shaft of the upper roll revolves in sliding journals, so that the rolls adjust themselves to the varying thickness of the goods. The mangle is made so that it can be readily attached to any table, and is the only table mangle made that is reversible, so it can be operated by either right or left hand. It is geared to run smooth and easy, and being supplied with a suitable balance wheel is given a uniform and steady motion impossible to obtain by using a crank. It will do all plain work much better than can be done with flat irons and in one-quarter the time. Heretofore the price of mangles has kept many from purchasing. This objection has now been removed and we offer here a mangle with wood rolls, 23x3½ inches, first-class in every particular, and at a price within the means of all. It will last for years and more than save its cost each year. Our price is for mangle only. It can be used on any ordinary kitchen table. Shipping weight, 60 lbs. Price, $12.

No. 15639. This mangle is adapted for families, small hotels and laundries, restaurants, barber shops, etc.; it will do good work and will endure a ton pressure. It is furnished with a patent automatic table adjustment, mounted on casters, is double geared, with gear guard, and has our combination driving gear, causing it to turn easily under great pressure. The pressure is obtained by heavy coil springs at the end of the rolls and is easily adjusted; no heat, no fuel, no scorching in using this machine, and better results can be obtained than with irons; the rolls are made of hardwood chemically treated, and measure 24x6; the machine takes up a floor space of 21x30, and its shipping weight is 240 lbs. Price, $26.50.

OUR HOTEL MANGLE.

Indispensable to the economical management of any hotel or public institution.

No. 15640. This is our heavy machine and is especially adapted for use in hotels, laundries and institutes. It is built to sustain great pressure and is reinforced in all parts exposed to wear or strain. It is double geared, making the action of the rolls positive, and our combination driving gear is very light running. It is mounted on casters, and can be easily moved from place to place, and when not in use is readily set out of the way, occupying but little more room than a sewing machine. The gear is covered with a handsome guard, preventing the possibility of any danger to the operator. The machine is also fitted with an automatic table adjustment, which, being permanently attached to the machine, is not knocked about and marred or misplaced when needed. For use it is only necessary to raise the tables parallel with the rolls, and this device automatically secures them firmly in that position. In lowering them they are raised about ten degrees which releases the lock, and they can be lowered to the side of the machine. The rolls are hardwood, chemically treated, and measure 24x6 inches. The machine takes up a floor space of 23x30 inches, and its shipping weight is 260 lbs. Price, $33.60.

FOLDING WASH BENCHES.

No. 15648. Folding Double Wash Bench, made of hardwood and nicely finished. The upright piece is constructed so that any kind of a wringer can be fastened to it, and room enough each side of it for tubs. When not in use it may be folded up so it will occupy much less space than an ordinary wash bench. Weight, 25 lbs. Price, $1.54.

No. 15649. Tripod Wash Bench made of hard wood; very strong and durable, taking up less room than any other. Price, 25c.

LAP CUTTING BOARDS.

No. 15650. Lap Cutting Board, striped, oil finished and polished, with y measure stamped on it; size, 20x36 inches. Weigh' lbs. Each, 65c.
No. 15651. Lap Cutting Board, same shape 15650, made of white wood, plain, 20x36. Each, 5'

No difference how far away you live, we can save you a large proportion on a purchase.

The freight on 100 lbs. of hardware will be very little when you consider the saving. If you don't need hardware to make 100 lbs., add enough groceries to make up the weight.

Fig. 147. Washing machines, Sears, Roebuck and Co. catalogue, 1896. Reproduction courtesy Sears, Roebuck and Co.

machine but smooth, was in use in the 1860s and persisted well into the 20th century. An ingenious version was patented[19] in 1860 by **R.O. Meldrum and Amos B. Paxson** of East Hamburg, N.Y. In this (Fig. 148) the rollers were covered with rubber or leather and the upper roller was pressed down by an adjustable bow spring. A continuous canvas apron was passed between the rollers and stretched out to small idling rollers in front and behind. This served to carry the clothes into the wringer and out beyond the rollers

to fall into a suitable receptacle well clear of the wash tub.

Drying Clothes

The damp clothes from the wringer were usually hung outside to dry on a more or less horizontal cord, the clothesline. They were secured from falling by means of clothespins, which usually were wooden pegs with

Fig. 148. Clothes wringer, Meldrum-Paxson patent, 1860. Interpretation by LSR, based on the patent drawings.

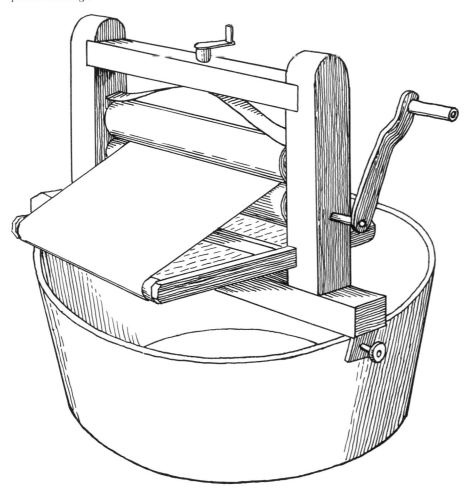

Fig. 149. Clothespin, hand-made. Black Creek Pioneer Village, Toronto.

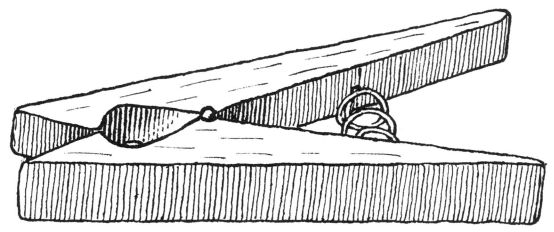

Fig. 150. Clothespin, Smith patent, 1853. Interpretation by LSR, based on the patent drawings.

a slot extending from one end to near the other (Fig. 149). This formed a kind of fork, which could be pushed down over the folded cloth and the line. For many years such wooden clothespins were carved at home, but later factory-made versions became available at moderate cost. In 1853, D.M. Smith of Springfield, Vermont, obtained a patent[20] for a different type of clothespin. It consisted of two strips of wood, pivoted on each other like small tongs, and held closed by a spring (Fig. 150). When the free ends were squeezed together, the closed ends opened, forming a pair of jaws that could be slipped over the cloth and the line.

Clamp-type clothespins of metal were also introduced at this time, but the wooden version, with various modifications of the spring, persisted into the 20th century. Today they are made of plastic, but they retain the essential principle of the 1853 invention.

No matter how tight the clothesline may have been stretched, it was likely to sag under a heavy load of clothes. The usual remedy was to prop it up near the middle with a pole of suitable length, having a forked end to engage the line, or perhaps only a bent nail projecting near the end. Greater stability was provided by using two poles crossed at their upper ends to form a notch for the line.

WILLARD'S PORTABLE CLOTHES BAR.

Fig. 151. Laundry drying rack, Willard patent, 1862. Scientific American, new series, vol. 6, 1862, p. 152. *Photograph courtesy the Metropolitan Toronto Library Board.*

The clothesline pulley was an added convenience. With the aid of two wooden, later metal, pulleys a clothesline in the form of a long loop could be strung from house to post or tree. The person hanging the damp clothes could stand at one end and not have to move the laundry basket with its load. As each article was hung on the lower section of the loop, the line was pushed away, bringing more line around from the upper side and into position for the next piece of clothing.

Cold weather did not prevent clothes from drying outside. In fact, the combination of frost and sunshine helped to bleach white cloth. But handing wet clothes in cold weather is uncomfortable, and the drying of a small "wash" was often done inside. This could be done using a clothesline reel, or on a rack of wooden bars. In 1862 H. Willard of Vergennes, Vermont, obtained a patent[22] for a rack that could be hung on a wall, with the bars hinged at one end so that they could be folded up when not in use (Fig. 151). Another form of rack was of wire, and was attached to the stovepipe above the stove, so as to take advantage of the heat. Small items, such as stockings or towels, were dried on such a device (Fig. 27).

Ironing

Most clothes and bedding were ironed after drying. This involved pressing the cloth by passing a hot weight ("iron") over the surface. It was another fatiguing operation, especially in hot weather. During the years when the open fireplace provided kitchen heat, the irons could not be heated directly over the fire without becoming dirty. The

Fig. 152. Hollow iron with core, LSR Collection.

Fig. 153. Sad-iron, LSR Collection.

problem was solved by using a hollow iron, into which a heated block of metal or brick could be introduced (Fig. 152). The opening in these irons is at the rear of the triangular body, with a vertical sliding or a swing door to hold the block in place.

With the advent of the cooking stove, the problem of keeping the face of the iron clean was no longer serious, and irons came into general use that consisted of a solid block of metal with a permanently attached horizontal handle (Fig. 153). These were called sad-irons; the word "sad" apparently means solid. The handle may be sheathed in wood, but if not, it must have been grasped

with a cloth pad for insulation. The shape of the earlier box iron was retained, with pointed front end, and sides curving convexly to the wide, square rear end.

In 1852 the self-heating "smoothing-iron" was introduced in the patent[23] of Nicholas Taliaferro of Augusta and William Cummings of Murphysville, Kentucky. Examples of this and many other self-heating irons are preserved in collections (Fig. 154). They are hollow, with a detachable lid, bearing an insulated handle and a curved pipe for ventilation. Burning charcoal was introduced to heat the body of the iron. In early models the pipe projected forward, but

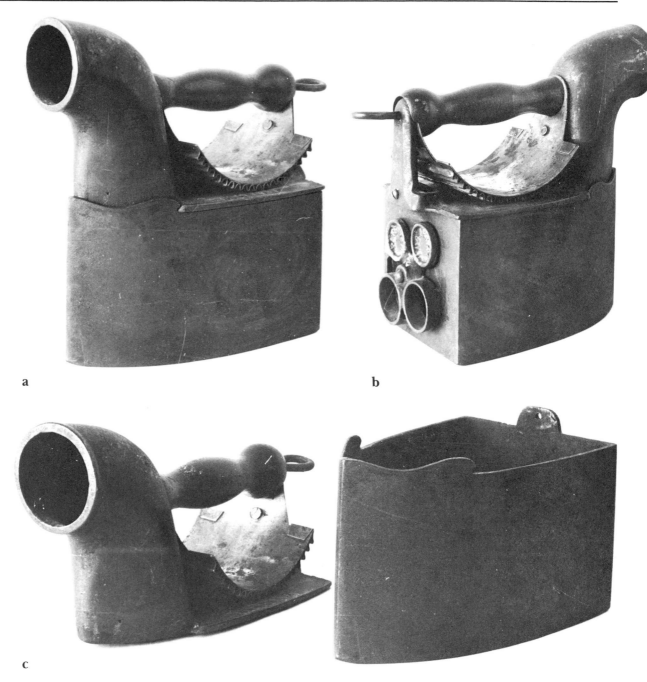

a

b

c

Fig. 154. Self-heating iron with built-in crimper, Hagerty patent, 1896: (a) front view, closed; (b) rear view, closed; (c) front view with lid removed. Black Creek Pioneer Village, Toronto.

in others it was turned to the right side, away from the operator, or eliminated completely. In some of these irons the fuel consisted of coke pellets instead of charcoal. Self-heating irons are large and heavy and were used mainly in commercial laundries.

It was obvious by the middle of the 19th century that a sad-iron with a detachable handle would be much more practical than one with a fixed handle, so that a number of irons could be heated on the stove, and used and replaced in turn with the same handle, which would remain cool. Various means of attachment were tried, but the junction was either too loose, or required too much time to secure. The problem was solved in 1871 by Mrs. Mary Florence Potts of Ottumwa, Iowa, who had already patented[24] the double-pointed sad-iron to utilize the back stroke as well as the forward motion.

Mrs. Pott's second patent[25] involved the double-pointed iron, but the top had a deep hollow (Fig. 155). Over this was screwed a lid, with an opening smaller than the diameter of the cavity, and with a transverse bar across the middle of the opening.

Fig. 155. *Sad-iron, Florence Potts patents, 1870, 1871: (a) assembled iron; (b) top of body showing* *attachment-point for handle. LSR Collection.*

a

b

The main part of the handle was a semicircle of wood, with a horizontal iron bar joining the ends. In this bar was a spring-loaded, claw-like clamp, which could be raised easily with the first two fingers while holding the handle with the thumb and other fingers. Placed in position and with the claw released, the handle was secured to the body of the iron

Fig. 156. Sad-iron with detachable handle, Jas. Smart Mfg. Co., Brockville, Ontario: (a) with handle attached; (b) with handle removed. LSR Collection.

a

b

by a firm grip of the claw under the transverse strip of the lid. The Potts iron rapidly achieved widespread popularity. Early examples were made by the Enterprise Manufacturing Company of Philadelphia, but later these irons were produced by many other firms, including some in Canada. The Potts iron continued in wide use into the 20th century, and was sold in Europe as well as North America. It is still useful in areas where electric power is not available.

Other types of sad-iron with detachable handle appeared in the later decades of the 19th century, but none was as popular as the original Potts design. The Jas. Smart Mfg. Co. of Brockville, Ontario, made an iron with the body similar to that of the Potts iron, but with a straight handle, and a clamp that is released by pressing forward with the thumb on a wire lever (Fig. 156). In 1887 Nelson B. Streeter of Groton, N.Y., patented[26] what he called the Sensible iron; it has a solid body, with a hook-like projection upward at the front end and a vertical wire loop behind (Fig. 157). The handle, which is straight, has a projection at the rear to fit under the loop, and a spring-loaded lever in front, which engages the projection on the body, and can be released by pushing forward with the thumb. The Sensible iron came in various sizes for different kinds of garments, and there was even an elongated version for sleeves (Fig. 158).

The so-called Asbestos iron appeared in the late 1890s, a product of the Dover Manufacturing Co. of Dover, Ohio.[27] In 1900 a patent[28] for this type of sad-iron was issued to Ole Tverdahl and L.D. Clark of Stoughton, Wisconsin. In this the body of the iron is double-pointed and solid, and has a projecting ledge around the lower rim (Fig. 159). There is a small hole on each side of the iron, just below the top. The handle is of wood, and is attached by a curved metal piece to the "skirt", a metal shell shaped to fit over the main part of the iron body. In some versions this shell is lined with asbestos, hence the name. A piece of spring metal, shaped like an inverted "U" is pivoted on two pins in holes on the sides of the skirt. When the spring is in the vertical position, the two

a

b

Fig. 157. "Sensible" iron, Streeter patent, 1887: (a) with handle attached; (b) with handle removed. LSR Collection.

pins are spread apart. The skirt can be slipped over the iron body and the spring pushed to one end of the handle. This releases the pressure on the spring, and allows the pins to engage the holes on the sides of the iron body and so provide a firm grip. The

Fig. 158. "Sensible" iron shaped for ironing sleeves, Black Creek Pioneer Village, Toronto.

advantage of the Asbestos iron was in the insulation it provided between the hot body and the operator's hand.

The goffering iron is a device that goes back to the 16th century, but which continued in use through the 19th and into the 20th century. The name is derived from the French word *gaufrer*, to crimp, and the iron was used to put the crimping or fluting on lace collars and cuffs. Later it served to make the ruffles on shirts. The usual goffering iron (Fig. 160) is an iron cylinder about an inch in diameter, with a blunt point at one end and an opening to the hollow interior at the other. It is supported on some sort of stand, with a metal or wooden base and an upright, usually an S-curved rod. In use the iron was heated by introducing a hot metal rod into the interior. The cloth to be crimped was previously soaked in a starch soluton and allowed to dry partially. It was bent over the curved surface of the heated iron and pressed down. By repeating this at intervals a series of

ruffles was produced that would remain until the next laundering.

The folds produced by the goffering iron had to be made one at a time, and the fluting could not be finer than the relatively large diameter of the cylinder. In the 1860s the fluting iron appeared, a device for making ruffles on a small scale and many folds at a time. An excellent account of fluting irons is given by Glissman.[29] The simplest, if not the earliest, was patented[30] in 1866 by C.A. Sterling of New York, N.Y. (Fig. 161). This consists of two parts, a rectangular plate of iron, the upper surface of which is corrugated, and a curved plate with handle corrugated on its lower surface to fit the flat plate. In use, the flat plate was heated, the starched fabric laid over it, and the curved plate rocked over cloth and corrugations to produce the fluting. The Sterling fluter was manufactured by W.H. Howell Co. of Geneva, Illinois, and was sold under the name of Geneva Hand Fluter. It is iliustrated in the Sears, Roebuck catalogue of 1897. A similar fluter was manufactured by Smart & Sheppard of Brockville, Ontario.

Combination fluting and conventional irons were made in the 1880s by attaching the fixed plate of the fluter to the side of the iron body. The other portion of the fluter, with handle, was similar to that of the Sterling fluter, and was separate from the iron body.

Mechanical fluters appeared in the 1866 patents[31] of Susan R. Knox and S.R. Corriston of New York, N.Y. These were a kind of miniature wringer, but with rollers having interlocking corrugations (Fig. 162). Heat was provided by introducing a hot-iron rod into the upper roller. The cloth to be fluted was slipped between the two rollers, which were turned by means of a crank attached to the lower roller.

The smoothing board was a device of European origin but used by the Pennsyl-vania Germans and Mennonites in both the United States and Canada. It is a long, narrow board with a handle on the top surface or at one end (Fig. 163). The under surface is flat or slightly convex, and may be smooth or transversely corrugated. The smooth form was used with a simple wooden roller, on which the damp cloth was wound. Smoothing was done by working the board back and forth over the roller and cloth. The corrugated board was used without the roller by drawing the under surface across the cloth on a flat, padded table.

In the more elaborate households the ironing of large textiles, such as sheets, was done by means of a mangle. In its early form this consisted of two or three large wooden rollers, weight-loaded with iron or stones above, which were revolved over a flat bed of wood by means of a crank. The cloth, folded to fit, was fed under the rollers, the pressure of which flattened the wrinkles

Fig. 159. "Asbestos" iron, Tverdahl-Clark patent, 1900. LSR Collection.

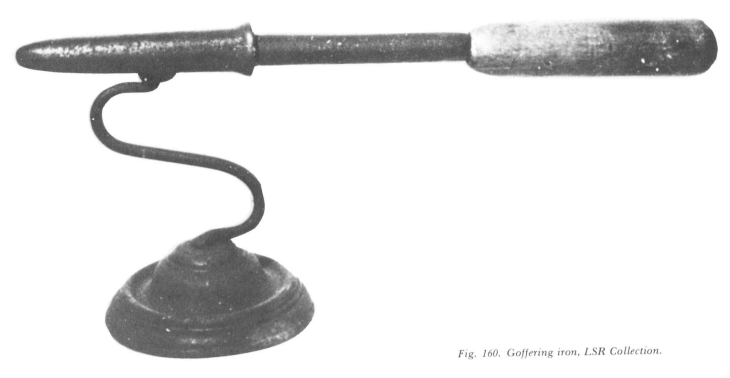

Fig. 160. Goffering iron, LSR Collection.

Fig. 161. Fluting iron, Sterling patent, 1866. Black
Creek Pioneer Village, Toronto.

Fig. 162. Fluting machine, Susan R. Knox patent, 1866. Black Creek Pioneer Village, Toronto.

and folds. The first U.S. patent[32] for a mangle was issued to R.A. Stratton of Philadelphia, in 1857. This had four rollers of metal, one above and two below, spring-loaded, and an intermediary roller on which the clothes were wound. Most of the later mangles had a flat bed with one roller above and one below, and a fly wheel and gear drive (Fig. 164). The Sears, Roebuck catalogue of 1897 shows three styles of mangle, the small, table-top model for use by families, the larger for hotels. One of the advantages listed for the mangle was

the absence of heat, with less chance of damage to the cloth.

Ironing was usually done on a table, padded with some sort of heavy fabric, such as an old blanket, and covered with flannelette. In larger households, with servants, the ironing table might be permanently set up. The top was long and narrow, and two persons could work on it together. In ordinary homes, however, the kitchen table, temporarily padded, would have to serve. The first U.S. patent[33] for a special ironing table

Fig. 163. Smoothing board. Black Creek Pioneer Village, Toronto.

Fig. 164. Mangle. Kitchen in restored King house, Woodside National Historic Site, Kitchener, Ontario.

Vandenburg & Harvey,

Ironing Table,

Nº 19,390,   *Patented Feb. 16, 1858.*

Fig. 1

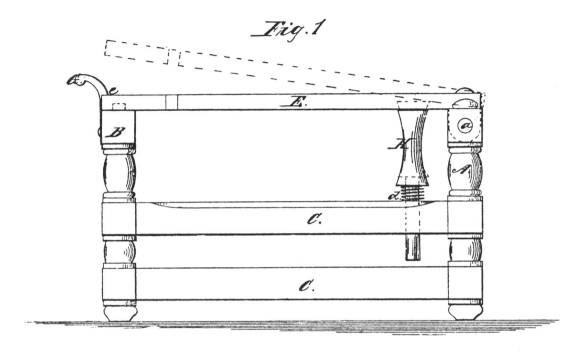

Fig. 2

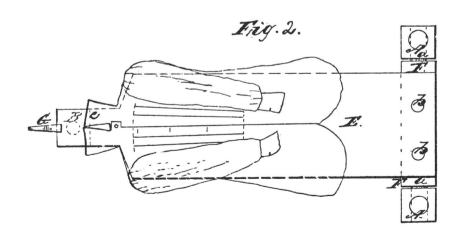

*Fig. 165. Ironing table, Vandenberg-Harvey patent,
1858. U.S. patent drawings.*

was issued to W. Vandenberg and J. Harvey of New York, N.Y., in 1858. This (Fig. 165) consisted of a narrow table top, hinged at one end to allow the garment to be slipped over it. Modifications of the idea were patented by the same inventors, also in 1858. This ironing table was the forerunner of the familiar folding "ironing board", which is still in use.

The Bath

A delightful account of bathing facilities since ancient times has been given by Wright.[34] Cleanliness of the body, at least since Roman times, seems to have lagged behind housecleaning and laundry as one of the near-godly virtues. In fact, until well into the 19th century there was a common belief that frequent bathing led to debility and nervous disorders. By the mid-century, however, the Saturday night bath was a widespread custom, and washing the feet might be done every evening, as much as anything to protect the bedding from being soiled. The weekly ablution was commonly performed in the ordinary wash-tub, wood or metal, and the water for the bath heated on the stove. In fact, the kitchen might well have to double as the bathroom once a week.

With the development of skill in sheet-metal working, bathing vessels of various shapes and functions appeared in the 1850s and persisted into the 20th century (Fig. 166). Among the common survivors is the sponge bath, a shallow vessel about three feet in diameter. The central portion is relatively deep, with vertical sides; around this is a wide, flaring rim to catch the splash. At one point on the rim is a small platform with one or two outside supporting legs. This served as a seat for the bather, although sponge baths were commonly taken standing up.

The sitz or sit bath was shaped like a large coal scuttle, and was intended for bathing the hip region. The user sat in it, with legs dangling out the low side. The foot bath was a small tub-shaped vessel about a foot and half in diameter. In contrast, the true bathtub or plunge bath was an elongate receptacle, shaped much like the modern bath tub, and measuring up to six feet in length. Here at last was a bath in which one could practice total immersion.

All of these baths were made of sheet metal, usually zinc, but copper and enameled iron were also used. Baths permanently set up in a bathroom were usually of wood with a metal lining. In these some type of water source and drainage could be installed. One of the earliest ideas for such an arrangement appears in the 1853 U.S. patent[35] of J.L. Mott, New York, N.Y., in which provision is made to admit both hot and cold water to the tub in the desired proportions. This was a forecast of the modern bathtub with separate taps for hot and cold water to emerge through a single opening.

Shower baths were the subject of invention well before the patented bathtubs. A "portable" shower bath was patented[36] in 1843 by Nathaniel Waterman of Boston, Mass. (Fig. 167). It consisted of a closed cylindrical vessel with perforated bottom, which was partly filled by placing it in the bath water. A valve in the lid was then closed and the whole vessel elevated by the bather and held overhead. The valve was opened by pulling down on a rod, allowing air to enter and the water to fall onto the bather.

A less portable type of shower bath appeared in the 1843 patent[37] of Stephen Bates, Dedham, Mass. In this the shower water was placed in a pivoted vessel, which could be tipped over a perforated plate, allowing the water to fall on the bather. The whole arrangement was mounted in a frame so that it could be raised and lowered on pulleys. The bather could lower the receptacle to refill it for repeated use.

An interesting aspect of these two shower-bath patents is that they imply a common previous use of this kind of bath.

Bathing facilities with hot and cold running water were restricted for a long time to those who could afford their own hot water system. But by the 1890s such luxuries, thanks to gas heaters and municipal water systems, were within reach of families with moderate incomes.

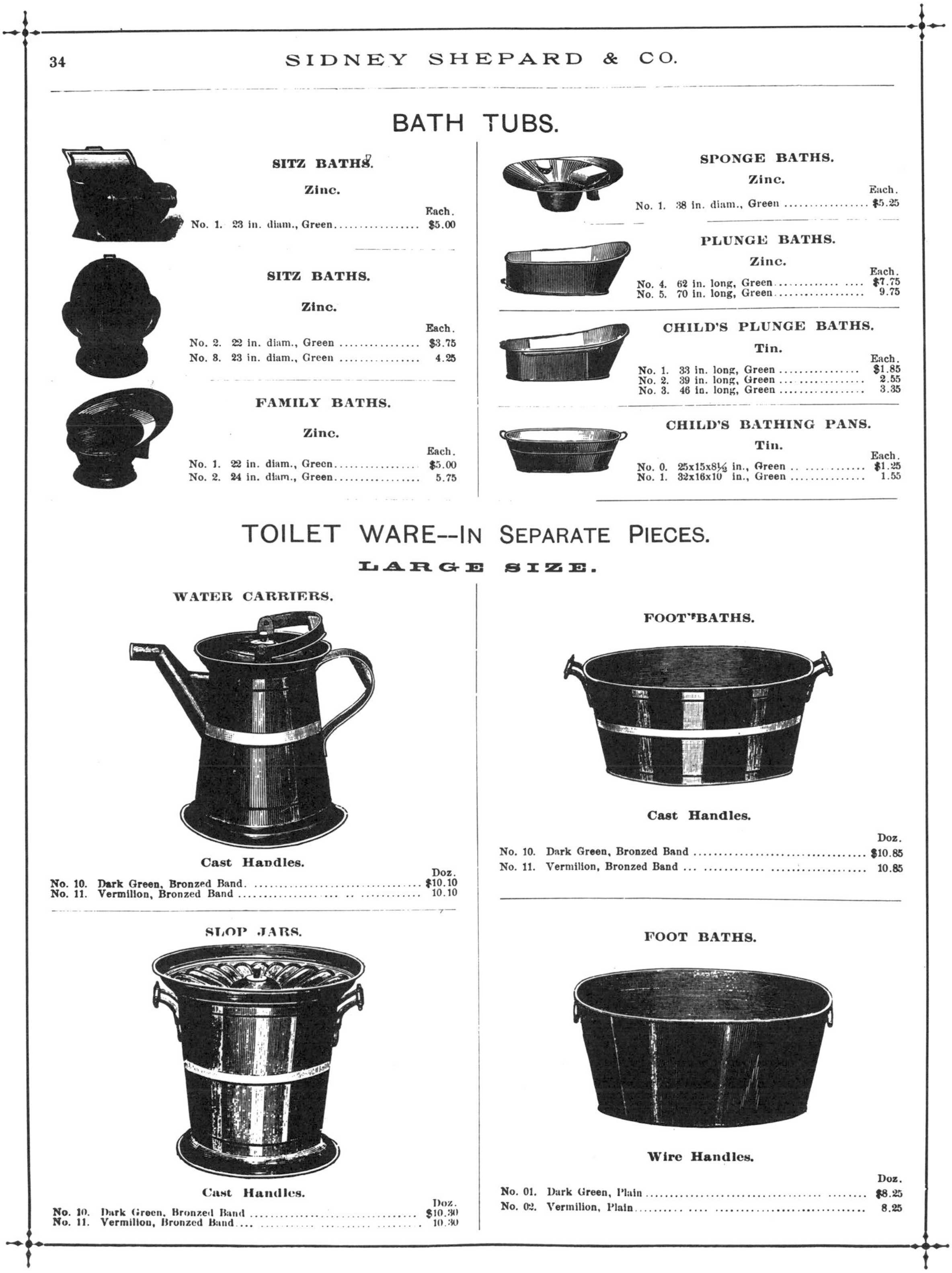

34

SIDNEY SHEPARD & CO.

BATH TUBS.

SITZ BATHS.

Zinc.

		Each.
No. 1.	23 in. diam., Green	$5.00

SITZ BATHS.

Zinc.

		Each.
No. 2.	22 in. diam., Green	$3.75
No. 3.	23 in. diam., Green	4.25

FAMILY BATHS.

Zinc.

		Each.
No. 1.	22 in. diam., Green	$5.00
No. 2.	24 in. diam., Green	5.75

SPONGE BATHS.

Zinc.

		Each.
No. 1.	38 in. diam., Green	$5.25

PLUNGE BATHS.

Zinc.

		Each.
No. 4.	62 in. long, Green	$7.75
No. 5.	70 in. long, Green	9.75

CHILD'S PLUNGE BATHS.

Tin.

		Each.
No. 1.	33 in. long, Green	$1.85
No. 2.	39 in. long, Green	2.55
No. 3.	46 in. long, Green	3.35

CHILD'S BATHING PANS.

Tin.

		Each.
No. 0.	25x15x8½ in., Green	$1.25
No. 1.	32x16x10 in., Green	1.55

TOILET WARE--IN SEPARATE PIECES.

LARGE SIZE.

WATER CARRIERS.

Cast Handles.

		Doz.
No. 10.	Dark Green, Bronzed Band	$10.10
No. 11.	Vermilion, Bronzed Band	10.10

SLOP JARS.

Cast Handles.

		Doz.
No. 10.	Dark Green, Bronzed Band	$10.30
No. 11.	Vermilion, Bronzed Band	10.30

FOOT BATHS.

Cast Handles.

		Doz.
No. 10.	Dark Green, Bronzed Band	$10.85
No. 11.	Vermilion, Bronzed Band	10.85

FOOT BATHS.

Wire Handles.

		Doz.
No. 01.	Dark Green, Plain	$8.25
No. 02.	Vermilion, Plain	8.25

Fig. 166. Bath tubs and bathing equipment, catalogue of Sidney Shepard & Co., Buffalo, New York, 1888. Courtesy of The Henry Ford Museum, Dearborn, Michigan.

The Water Closet

The little house at the back of the garden was an almost universal part of the domestic establishment in rural North America until well into the 20th century. In the spacious environment of the farm this might be a practical if inconvenient arrangement. But in the city it was objectionable as the source of odors and contamination, and for the necessity of the periodical removals of the accumulated "night soil". The development of the modern water closet and other devices for sanitary disposal were urban events, associated with a higher standard of living and the availability of a community water supply.

According to Wright,[38] the first practical water closet was patented by Alexander Cummings of London, England, in 1775. This combined an overhead reservoir for the water, a bowl with a sliding-valve outlet, and an S-curved drain pipe to act as a water trap and a siphon. The bowl was flushed by pulling up a handle, which released water into the bowl and opened the outlet valve.

In 1778 Joseph Bramah of London modified the Cummings invention by substituting a hinged valve for the sliding valve. This version was manufactured in large quantities until late in the 19th century, and must have been exported to North America for use in the more elegant residences and hotels.

By the middle of the 19th century various types of water closet were being made in the United States. The first U.S. patent for a water closet was issued to J. Stone of New York, N.Y., in 1835, but it was not until 1847 that another such patent[39] appeared, granted to James Ingram and James Stuart, also of New York City. Their device was similar to the Bramah water closet except that there were two hinged valves, one open when the other was closed. During the 1850s a number of ingenious and complex improvements on the water closet were patented. Some of these had the operating parts connected to the seat, opening the flushing valve when relieved of the occupant's weight. By the 1870s most city people of the middle and upper income groups had water closets in their homes. The happy state described in the Kansas City song* from the musical comedy *Oklahoma!* had been achieved long before the turn of the century.

A short-lived rival of the water closet was the earth closet, invented in 1860 by Henry Moule, an English clergyman.[40] It achieved some popularity in the United States during the 1870s, partly due to the strong

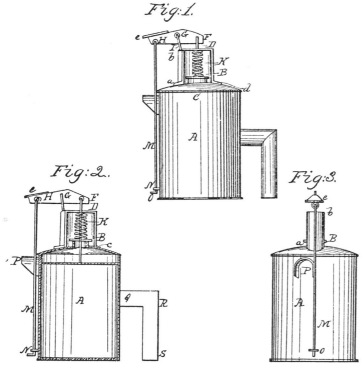

Fig. 167. Shower bath, Waterman patent, 1843. U.S. patent drawing.

*"You can walk to privies in the rain and never wet your feet."

advocacy of the Beecher sisters in their "American Women's Home".[41] In the earth closet a layer of earth was dropped into the receptacle, either by pulling a lever or by releasing the seat. Good sanitation and freedom from odor were claimed for this device. A number of U.S. patents for improvements on earth toilets were issued in the 1870s, indicating a strong, if brief, interest. Curiously, the principle has been revived in recent years for use in the rural homes and summer cottages, using a chemically treated "earth".

Another substitute for the water closet where running water and sewers were not available was the chemical closet. This had a receptacle containing water treated with some chemical such as "chlorinated lime" to suppress odors. Of course it had to be emptied periodically into an adjacent sump, so it was no great improvement over the old privy down the path.

Epilogue

Three major events directed the transformation of the almost medieval 18th-century menage into the domestic technology of the 20th century. The first of these was the displacement of the fireplace by the cooking stove, beginning in the 1840s. The second was the introduction of municipal water systems and sewage disposal, extending from the 1850s until well into the 20th century. The third was mainly a 20th-century event, the electrification of the household. The electric light became a domestic appliance in the 1880s, and this fostered the development of electrical distribution systems, but it remained for the early 20th century to see the long-distance transmission of power from hydro-electric generating plants, placing electric appliances within the means of most city families. The other factor in the electrification of the home was the development of the small alternating-current motor. This could be applied to the washing machine, the vacuum cleaner, the sewing machine, the refrigerator, and a host of stirrers and grinders. Purely as a source of heat the electric current could be used for stoves, irons, toasters, and space heaters.

Eventually electric power distribution spread out from the cities to the country, and brought with it all the conveniences of urban living, including hot and cold running water and a sewage disposal system. Later it helped to integrate country life into the world with the radio and television. The deep-freeze refrigerator provided a substitute for the chain-store grocery of the city. On dairy farms, electricity powered the milking machine and the cream separator, and pumped water for the drinking trough.

Modern life, some say, is too complex; we should return to the simple life style of our ancestors. But the study of 19th-century domestic appliances, if it shows nothing else, reveals a constant struggle for improvement, with each innovation, if successful, being gratefully adopted by willing users. If the "good old days" were all that idyllic, there would have been no such demand for improvements. Obviously the people of those days did not consider their way of life to be the best-possible world. They sought something better, and in the process created a unique legacy of material well-being that should inspire deep gratitude but not necessarily nostalgia.

Notes

Introduction

1. Leggett, 1874.
2. Annual Report U.S. Commissioner of Patents for 1850, Washington, D.C., 1851.
3. List of Canadian Patents from the beginning of the Patent Office, June, 1824, to the 31st of August, 1872, Ottawa, 1882.

Chapter One

1. Christy, 1926, pp. 11-16.
2. U.S. Patent (no number), May 6, 1820.
3. U.S. Patent No. 63,753, April 9, 1867.
4. U.S. Patent (no number), March 20, 1820.

Chapter Two

1. Wright, 1964, p. 114.
2. U.S. Patent No. 455, November 4, 1837.
3. U.S. Patent No. 1,333, September 20, 1839.
4. U.S. Patent (no number), February 24, 1812.
5. Canadian Patent No. 153, June 1, 1835.
6. U.S. Patent No. 304, June 29, 1837.
7. Clegg, 1853.
8. U.S. Patent No. 12,434, February 27, 1855.
9. U.S. Patent No. 63,815, April 16, 1867.
10. U.S. Patent No. 70,641, November 5, 1867.
11. U.S. Patent No. 47,529, May 2, 1865.
12. U.S. Patent No. 21,845, October 19, 1858.
13. U.S. Patent No. 21,416, September 7, 1858.
14. U.S. Patent No. 21,387, August 31, 1858.
15. U.S. Patent No. 19,827, April 6, 1858.

Chapter Three

1. U.S. Patent No. 496,756, May 2, 1893.
2. U.S. Patent No. 496,809, May 2, 1893.
3. U.S. Patent No. 47,875, May 23, 1865.
4. U.S. Patent No. 52,449, February 6, 1866.
5. U.S. Patent No. 23,262, March 15, 1859.
6. U.S. Patent No. 23,246, March 15, 1859.
7. U.S. Patents: No. 591,575, October 12, 1897; No. 626,212, May 30, 1899. Canadian Patent No. 58,029, November 6, 1897.
8. Canadian Patent No. 72,917, August 27, 1901. U.S. Patent No. 694,704, March 4, 1902.
9. U.S. Patent No. 4,149, August 16, 1845.
10. U.S. Patents: No. 104,537, June 21, 1870; No. 143,867, October 21, 1873.
11. U.S. Patent No. 23,694, April 19, 1859.
12. U.S. Patent No. 39,134, July 7, 1863.
13. U.S. Patent No. 463,818, November 24, 1891.
14. U.S. Patent No. 350,023, September 28, 1886.
15. U.S. Patent No. 332,375, December 15, 1885.
16. U.S. Patent No. 193,220, June 15, 1877.
17. U.S. Patent (no number), February 14, 1803.
18. U.S. Patent (no number), August 25, 1809.
19. U.S. Patent No. 686, April 13, 1838.
20. U.S. Patent No. 6,789, October 16, 1849.
21. U.S. Patents: No. 15,603, August 26, 1856; No. 16,104, November 18, 1856.
22. U.S. Patents: No. 16,417, January 13, 1857; No. 16,666, February 17, 1857.
23. U.S. Patent No. 59,884, November 20, 1866.
24. U.S. Patent No. 93,574, August 10, 1869.
25. U.S. Patents: No. 240,893, May 3, 1881; No. 241,107, May 3, 1881; No. 251,982, January 3, 1882; No. 273,418, March 6, 1883.
26. U.S. Patent No. 15,683, September 9, 1856.
27. U.S. Patent No. 15,133, June 17, 1856.
28. U.S. Patent No. 32, 561, June 18, 1861.
29. U.S. Patent No. 44,044, August 30, 1864.
30. U.S. Patent No. 37,038, December 2, 1862.
31. U.S. Patent No. 124,272, March 5, 1872.
32. U.S. Patent No. 147,559, February 17, 1874.

33. U.S. Patent No. 252,670, January 24, 1882.
34. U.S. Patent No. 260,756, July 11, 1882.
35. U.S. Patent No. 87,322, March 2, 1869.
36. U.S. Patent No. 103,830, June 7, 1870.
37. U.S. Patents: No. 122,305, January 2, 1872; No. 125,004, March 26, 1872.
38. U.S. Patent No. 9,558, January 25, 1853.
39. U.S. Patent No. 409,111, August 13, 1889.
40. U.S. Patent No. 26,640, December 27, 1859.
41. U.S. Patent No. 28,310, May 15, 1860.
42. U.S. Patent No. 28,973, July 3, 1860.
43. U.S. Patent No. 100,348, March 1, 1870.
44. U.S. Patent No. 40,604, November 17, 1863.
45. U.S. Patent No. 54,797, May 15, 1866.
46. U.S. Patent No. 63,716, April 9, 1867.
47. U.S. Patent No. 103,802, May 31, 1870.
48. U.S. Patent No. 538,905, May 7, 1895.
49. U.S. Patent No. 539,664, May 21, 1895.
50. U.S. Patent No. 536,778, April 2, 1895.
51. U.S. Patent No. 591,322, October 5, 1897.
52. U.S. Patent No. 596,362, December 28, 1897.
53. U.S. Patent No. 11,351, July 25, 1854.
54. U.S. Patent No. 458,041, August 18, 1891.
55. U.S. Patent No. 571,218, July 31, 1896.
56. U.S. Patent No. 28,967, July 3, 1860.
57. U.S. Patent No. 35,554, June 10, 1862.
58. U.S. Patent No. 61,251, January 15, 1867.
59. U.S. Patent No. 5,945, November 28, 1848.
60. U.S. Patent No. 20,815, July 6, 1858.
61. U.S. Patent No. 5,601, May 30, 1848.
62. U.S. Patent No. 5,960, December 12, 1848.
63. U.S. Patents: No. 128,856, July 9, 1872; No. 165,545, July 13, 1875.
64. Gould, 1958, p. 124.
65. Canadian Patent No. 2191, January 5, 1867.
66. Canadian Patent No. 4177, December 15, 1874.
67. U.S. Patent No. 5,560, May 9, 1848.

Chapter Four

1. British Patent No. 1425, July 3, 1784.

2. British Patent No. 4388, December 24, 1819.
3. U.S. Patent No. 2,703, July 2, 1842.
4. U.S. Patent No. 14,806, May 6, 1856.
5. U.S. Patent No. 7,921, February 4, 1851.
6. U.S. Patent No. 2,604, May 4, 1842.
7. U.S. Patent No. 11,497, August 8, 1854.
8. U.S. Patent No. 11,663, August 29, 1854.
9. U.S. Patent No. 3,028, April 6, 1843.
10. U.S. Patent (no number), October 16, 1830.
11. Canadian Patent No. 25, October 3, 1831.
12. U.S. Patent No. 10,099, October 4, 1853.
13. U.S. Patent No. 13,860, November 27, 1855.
14. U.S. Patent No. 33,047, August 13, 1861.
15. U.S. Patent No. 36,680, October 14, 1862.
16. U.S. Patent No. 39,320, July 21, 1863.
17. U.S. Patent No. 135,749, February 11, 1873.
18. U.S. Patent No. 49,984, September 19, 1865.
19. U.S. Patent No. 37,867, March 10, 1863.
20. U.S. Patent No. 292,114, January 15, 1884.
21. U.S. Patent No. 30,466, October 23, 1860.
22. U.S. Patent No. 40,566, November 10, 1863.
23. U.S. Patents: No. 125, April 23, 1872; No. 134,542, January 7, 1873; No. 142,103, August 26, 1873; No. 145,176, December 2, 1873. Canadian Patent No. 3138, February 24, 1874.
24. Canadian Patent No. 24,994, September 27, 1886. U.S. Patent No. 359,968, March 22, 1887.
25. Clegg, 1853.
26. U.S. Patents: Nos. 377,698, 377,699, 377,700, 377,701, February 7, 1888.
27. Canadian Patent No. 10,654, November 17, 1879. U.S. Patent No. 223,898, January 27, 1880.
28. Schroeder, 1923, pp. 60-62.
29. Barham, 1912, p. 26; Schroeder, 1923, p. 56.
30. Barham, 1912, p. 135; Schroeder, 1923, p. 85.

Chapter Five

1. U.S. Patent No. 14,482, March 18, 1856.

2. U.S. Patent No. 70,622, November 5, 1867.
3. Canadian Patent No. 14,334, March 6, 1882.
4. U.S. Patent No. 251,381, December 27, 1881.
5. U.S. Patent No. 334,915, January 26, 1886.
6. U.S. Patent No. 10,143, October 18, 1853.
7. U.S. Patent No. 47,935, May 30, 1865.
8. U.S. Patent No. 595,845, December 21, 1897. Canadian Patent No. 58,772, January 21, 1898.
9. U.S. Patent No. 10,509, February 7, 1854.
10. U.S. Patent No. 2,466, February 21, 1842.
11. U.S. Patent No. 2,982, March 4, 1843.
12. U.S. Patent No. 35,252, May 13, 1863.
13. U.S. Patent No. 7,622, September 3, 1850.
14. U.S. Patent No. 6,009, February 6, 1849.
15. U.S. Patent No. 16,234, December 16, 1856.
16. U.S. Patent No. 7,931, February 11, 1851.
17. U.S. Patent No. 4,750, September 10, 1846.
18. U.S. Patent No. 7,776, November 12, 1850.
19. U.S. Patent No. 8,296, August 12, 1851.
20. U.S. Patent No. 9,041, June 15, 1852.
21. U.S. Patent No. 8,284, August 12, 1851.
22. U.S. Patent No. 61,270, January 15, 1867.
23. Canadian Patent No. 1181, January 16, 1861.
24. The Globe, Toronto, Canada West, May 11, 1855.
25. The Daily News, Kingston, Canada West, July 22, 1861.
26. Great Western Gazetteer, Commercial Advertiser, and Business Directory, Toronto, Ontario, 1867, pp. 285-297.
27. U.S. Patent No. 19,612, March 9, 1858.
28. U.S. Patents: No. 22,320, November 30, 1858; No. 32,785, July 9, 1861; No. 32,925, July 30, 1861.
29. Canadian Patent No. 1433, April 18, 1872.

Chapter Six

1. U.S. Patent No. 9,160, July 27, 1852.
2. U.S. Patent No. 21,233, August 17, 1858.
3. U.S. Patent No. 182,346, September 19, 1876.
4. Lifshey, 1973, pp. 292-305.
5. U.S. Patent No. 621, March 3, 1838.
6. U.S. Patent No. 88,456, March 30, 1869.
7. U.S. Patent No. 7,288, April 16, 1850.
8. U.S. Patent No. 51,493, December 12, 1865.
9. U.S. Patent No. 272,288, February 13, 1883.
10. U.S. Patent No. 13,371, July 31, 1855.
11. Leggett, 1874.
12. Lower Canada Patent No. 1, July 8, 1824.
13. U.S. Patent No. 3,472, March 9, 1844.
14. U.S. Patent No. 3,654, July 9, 1844.
15. U.S. Patent No. 19,474, February 23, 1858.
16. Canadian Patent No. 20,725, December 13, 1884.
17. Canadian Patent No. 21,586, May 4, 1885.
18. U.S. Patent No. 5,106, May 8, 1847.
19. U.S. Patent No. 26,914, January 24, 1860.
20. U.S. Patent No. 10,163, October 25, 1853.
21. U.S. Patent No. 61,672, January 29, 1867.
22. U.S. Patent No. 34,456, February 18, 1862. Scientific American, n.s., vol. 6, p. 152, 1862.
23. U.S. Patent No. 8,848, March 20, 1852.
24. U.S. Patent No. 103,501, May 24, 1870.
25. U.S. Patent No. 113,448, April 4, 1871.
26. U.S. Patent No. 369,569, September 6, 1887.
27. Glissman, 1970, p. 88.
28. U.S. Patent No. 649,968, May 22, 1900.
29. Glissman, 1970, pp. 115-131.
30. U.S. Patent No. 57,403, August 21, 1866.
31. U.S. Patents: No. 53,633, April 3, 1866; No. 59,913, November 20, 1866.
32. U.S. Patent No. 16,887, March 24, 1857.
33. U.S. Patents: No. 19,390, February 16, 1858; No. 19,883, April 6, 1858; No. 20,231, May 11, 1858.
34. Wright, 1960, 1967.
35. U.S. Patent No. 10,049, September 27, 1853.
36. U.S. Patent No. 3,213, August 11, 1843.
37. U.S. Patent No. 3,302, October 12,, 1843.
38. Wright, 1960, p. 107.
39. U.S. Patent No. 4,926, January 13, 1847.
40. Wright, 1960, p. 208.
41. Beecher and Stowe, 1869.

Selected Bibliography

Abrahamson, Una. *God bless our home: Domestic life in nineteenth century Canada.* Toronto: Burns & MacEachern Ltd., 1966. 238 pages, illus.

Barham, G.B. *The development of the incandescent electric lamp.* London: Scott, Greenwood & Son, 1912. 198 pages, 25 figures, 2 plates.

Beecher, Catharine E. *A treatise on domestic economy, for the use of young ladies at home, and at school.* Boston: Marsh, Capon Lyon, and Webb, 1841. xxiv + 441 pages, illus.

Beecher, Catharine E., and Harriet B. Stowe. *The American woman's home: or, Principles of domestic science, . . .* New York: J.B. Ford & Co.; Boston: H.A. Brown & Co., 1869. 500 pages.

Child, Lydia M. *The American frugal housewife, dedicated to those who are not ashamed of economy.* Boston: Carter, Hendee, & Co., 16th ed., 1835. 130 pages, 1 plate.

Christy, Miller. *The Bryant and May Museum of Fire-making Appliances.* London: Bryant & May Ltd., 1926, 1928, 331 pages, 429 illus.

Clegg, Samuel, jr. *A practical treatise on the manufacture and distribution of coal gas, its introduction and progressive improvement.* London: John Weale, 2nd ed., 1853. 298 pages, 42 figures, 19 plates.

Cooper, Grace R. *The invention of the sewing machine.* Washington: Smithsonian Institution. U.S. National Museum, Bulletin 254, 1968, 156 pages, 136 figures.

Dover Stamping Co., 1869. *Tinware, tin toys, tinned iron wares, tinners' material, enameled stove hollow ware, tinners' tools and machines.* Illustrated catalogue and historical introduction. Princeton: The Pyne Press, 1971. 222 pages, illus.

Ewers, William, H.W. Baylor. *Sincere's history of the sewing machine.* Phoenix, Arizona: Sincere Press, 1970, 256 pages, illus., 1970.

Franklin, Linda C. *America in the kitchen from hearth to cookstove: An American domestic history of gadgets and utensils made or used in America from 1700 to 1920: A guide for collectors.* Florence, Alabama: House of Collectibles, Inc., 1976. xv + 271 pages, 1,155 figures.

Glissman, A.H. *The evolution of the sadiron.* Carlsbad, California: A.H. Glissman, 1970. 282 pages, illus.

Gould, Mary E. *Antique tin & tole ware: Its history and romance.* Rutland, Vermont: Charles E. Tuttle Co., 1958. xvi + 136 pages, frontis., 255 figures.

Langford, Laura Holloway. *The hearthstone; or life at home: A household manual. . . .* Philadelphia: Bradley & Co., 1883. 582 pages, illus.

Lantz, Louise K. *Old American kitchenware, 1725-1925.* Camden: Thos. Nelson Inc., 1970. 289 pages, illus.

Leggett, M.D. *Subject-matter index of patents of inventions issued by the United States Patent Office from 1790 to 1873, inclusive.* Washington: Government Printing Office, 1874. 3 vols., 1951 pages.

Lifshey, Earl. *The housewares story; a history of the American housewares industry.* Chicago: National Housewares Manufacturers Association, 1973. 384 pages, illus.

Lindsay, J.S. *Iron & brass implements of the English and American home.* Boston & London: The Medici Society, 1927. 211 pages, illus.

Mace, L.H., & Co. 1883. *Woodenware, meat safes, toys, refrigerators, children's carriages and house furnishing goods.* Illustrated catalogue and historical introduction. Princeton: The Pyne Press, 1971. 78 pages, illus.

Minhinnick, Jeanne. *At home in Upper Canada*. Toronto: Clark, Irwin & Co. Ltd., 1970. 228 pages, illus.

Norwak, Mary. *Kitchen antiques*. New York: Praeger Publishers, 1975. 135 pages, illus.

Putnam, Mrs. E. *Mrs. Putman's receipt book; and young housekeeper's assistant.* Boston: Ticknor, Reed, and Fields, 1855. 136 pages.

Rapp, H.W., jr. (ed.) *Early lighting; a pictorial guide*. The Rushlight Club, 1972. 129 pages, 456 figures.

Russell, L.S. *A heritage of light: Lamps and lighting in the early Canadian home*. Toronto: University of Toronto Press, 1968. 344 pages, 217 figures.

Schroeder, Henry. *History of electric light*. Washington: Smithsonian Institution. Smithson. Misc. Collec., vol. 76, no. 2, xiii + 95 pages, 96 figures.

Thuro, Catharine M.V. *Oil lamps; The kerosene era in North America*. Des Moines, Iowa: Wallace-Homestead Book Co., 1976. 352 pages, illus.

Thwing, Leroy. *Flickering flames: A history of domestic lighting through the ages*. Rutland, Vermont: Charles E. Tuttle Co., 1958. 138 pages, 53 figures, 96 plates.

Traill, Catharine P. *The female emigrant's guide, and hints on Canadian housekeeping*. Toronto: MacLear and Co., 1854. 271 pages, 8 figures.

Wheeler, R.G., *et. al. Mechanical arts at the Henry Ford Museum*. Dearborn, Michigan: The Edison Institute, 1974. 128 pages, illus.

Wright, Lawrence. *Clean and decent: The fascinating history of the bathroom & the water closet. . . .* London: Routledge & Kegan Paul, 1960. xii + 278 pages, illus.

Wright, Lawrence. *Home fires burning: The history of domestic heating and cooking*. London: Routledge & Kegan Paul, 1964. ix + 219 pages, illus.

General Index

(References in italic are figure numbers.)